Footprints in the Sand

A True Historical Sketch of when Northwest Michigan was inhabited by Indians, Mormons and Fishermen

By Stephen H. Smith

Edited by his Granddaughter Audrey S. Hilliker
And Great-Granddaughter Donna L. Heeres

Book Concern Printers
129 E. Franklin St., P.O. Box 330
Hancock, Michigan 49930
800-482-1250
www.BookConcernPrinters.com

Library of Congress Catalog Card Number:
ISBN 978-1-4507-5046-2

Table of Contents

Lives of great men all remind us
We can make our lives sublime,
And, departing, leave behind us
Footprints on the sand of time.

Footprints, that perhaps another,
Sailing o'er life's solemn main,
A forlorn and shipwrecked brother,
Seeing, shall take heart again.

Let us, then, be up and doing,
With a heart for any fate;
Still achieving, still pursuing,
Learn to labor and to wait.

From the poem "A Psalm of Life"
By Henry Wadsworth Longfellow, 1838

Travels of the Thomas Smith Family
April 1852 to October 1864

April 1852:	Left Detroit for Beaver Harbor. Thomas became Light Keeper for a year.
Spring 1853:	Thomas appointed Light Keeper at Illeaux Galets (Skille gul les).
Fall 1853:	Moved to Little Traverse (now Harbor Springs).
Spring 1854:	Moved to Pine River (now Charlevoix) and built a rough shelter.
June 1854:	Moved to Cross Village. Rented a house for a year, but stayed until after July 4, 1855. Thomas was elected Justice of the Peace in the Spring of 1855.
August 1855:	Moved to Middle Village. Built a good set of buildings, home and cooper shop.
Spring 1856:	Moved back to Pine River at the urging of friends there. Skirmish with the Mormons, later called the Battle of Pine River.
June 1856:	Moved to Little Traverse and rented a house. Treaty signed with the Indians and Federal Government, witnessed by young Stephen.
August 1856:	Moved back to Middle Village.
October 1862:	Moved to Yuba in Grand Traverse County.
October 1864:	Moved back to Pine River to take up homestead claim in Marion Township which he filed the spring before.

Foreword

When I was a little girl, I remember seeing my Grandfather busily writing on one after another of the lined, five-cent tablets from the grocery store, and was told that he was writing his "story." He finished it at the beginning of 1923, when he would have been almost seventy-four years old.

Later he went on to establish a neighborhood grocery store, and ran it successfully for several years. This store remained in the family for three generations, covering a period of fifty-eight years. After my grandmother passed on in 1929, he retired from the business, and lived with our family most of the next twelve years, until he died in 1941.

During those years that he lived with our family, I remember hearing him recount many times some of the interesting events which made up his story. I have read the manuscript several times in the years which have followed, but not until 1985 did it occur to me to try, with a minimum of editing, to make it available for publication. I felt people would be interested in what he had to share about the lives of the early pioneers of this region.

He had a typed copy made at one time, which I compared with the original tablets. My goal was to adhere as closely as possible to his own words, rearranging if necessary only when it emphasized or clarified the continuity of the narrative.

Although he felt himself the victim of a limited education, I was amazed at his vocabulary, spelling, grammar, punctuation, and scholarship in general. Truly he was a self-educated man, limited only in the sense of a formal education, as were many others of his generation.

Grandfather lived to be ninety two years old. Truly he did have to "learn to labor and to wait" as the poem says. But I am sure he would be gratified if now his work can reach and bless those who cherish the accounts of those early days in the history of northern Michigan.

In doing research into names, dates, places and events mentioned in the manuscript, I am grateful for assistance from librarians in several public libraries and Historical Societies. Also, material shared with me by Mr. Frank V. Phelps, King of Prussia, PA, on the genealogy of this branch of the Smith family has proved most helpful.

Audrey S. Hilliker, 1985

Chapter 1
A Query

Hello! Footprints in the sand! I wonder who could have made them?

Kind reader, if you have the interest and the necessary patience to follow this narrative through to the end, I will answer your query, and I will answer it truthfully, not only as to the places where these footprints were to be seen, but also the names of the people who made them and the dates when they were made.

I shall try to give you a fair, though brief, description of the conditions prevailing at the time, to help you to understand them as well as you can, and to note the marvelous changes this country has undergone in the brief time of a single life span.

To compensate you for your interest and the time you will devote to reading this narrative, I can say that much of this story has never been given to the public. Some of the events mentioned which have been reported by other writers are innocently incorrect, or in some cases, perhaps, have been purposely distorted or willfully falsified.

While I cannot claim, at this period of my life, to be the last surviving white person who was here in those early days, I was here on the day this story begins, and can testify from my own knowledge to the history, the adventure, the sentiment, the trials and hardships—but also the freedom and sublime grandeur of God's great open spaces in all their newness. All of these have been mine since long before our beautiful little cities were platted, before they were named, before they were peopled, and before the first inspiring thought had been shaped that made them real.

To be fair with you, as I have promised I would be, I must say that it is regrettable that neither I nor any other person, so far as I know, ever kept any diary of events as they transpired, so you will see I have to rely for the most part on my memory.

Generally, it is unsafe to depend on one's memory, especially where dates are concerned, but many dates can be verified in old family Bibles, books of account, business and other letters, notes—either paid or unpaid—and other miscellaneous data. With these to establish, with reasonable certainty, practically all of the dates, the others follow along in an orderly way.

Since I had no school and no playmates for most of these early years, nothing and nobody but a few grownups—fishermen and their wives—to divert or divide my attention from any circumstance or event, each became the subject of almost consuming interest to me, to be lived over and over many times each day and sometimes for many days in succession until some new thing of interest should occur. Thus these events became indelibly stamped on my memory as, indeed, they never could have been if my environment, my associations and my experiences had been such as are common to most other children.

So now, dear reader, you probably surmise that I left those footprints in the sand, and in that you are right. Or, at least, I left some of them—very naturally, the ones of the most importance to this story.

10

Chapter 2
The Northern Michigan Wilderness

There have been three events in my life which stand out as of much more than ordinary interest and importance to me. At least two of them changed the whole course of my life. All took place during the few years covered by this narrative, and two occurred during the same year.

The first important event of my life was when we left civilization on a fateful day in April, 1852, for a plunge into the wilderness of northern Michigan, where I should not be likely to see the inside of a schoolhouse or church, or any other public gathering place, until I should be grown to young manhood. And for most of that time, there was not a white boy or girl within fifty miles for a playmate.

I was born February 11, 1849 in the pretty little village of Redford, Wayne County, Michigan, about twelve miles northwest of Detroit. My father, Thomas Horatio Smith, was a man of good habits, thrifty, fairly intelligent with a fair education. He was a cooper by trade, industrious, a good workman and mechanic.

Down to the mid-1850's, Mackinac Island was the main shipping port and supply station of this entire region but as time went on, Beaver Island became a strong competitor. Having a beautiful harbor, being centrally located as to fishing grounds, surrounded by

11

several other islands, large and small, nearly all having good harbors, Beaver harbor was a most desirable location for a business of tremendous proportions.

It was also a regular stopping port for many of the steamers plying between Chicago and Milwaukee west, and Detroit, Cleveland and Buffalo east, thus making easy shipping to any market, and also making these cities easily accessible as markets in which to buy supplies. All of this made it not only a good place to operate a fish business, but a pleasant place in which to live.

In those days all fish were dressed and salted in hundred-pound half barrels. Knowing this, Father thought there would be an almost unlimited demand for barrels, and that he could do well here at his trade, all of which proved to be true.

So in April, 1852, he, my mother (Phebe Hull Smith) and I (at the age of three years) embarked from Detroit on the side-wheel steamer Michigan, bound for Beaver Island. Father was bringing himself and his family from the then, as now, largest city and

most improved part of the State, up here to a region of unbroken forests, without roads, schools, churches, libraries—many of these things which go to make up modern civilization.

The fishermen at this time were, for the most part, scattered up and down the shores of Lake Michigan. Bands of Indians roamed the region, although there were also some little settlements of Indians, numbering from two to a half dozen families, living deep in the forests, where they had their gardens and a few quiet villages on the lake shore.

What we soon found out was the fact that we were also entering a hotbed of Mormonism, with all its attendant crimes and horrors, for at that time on Beaver Island, and scattered somewhat among the other islands, was a considerable colony of Mormons, under the leadership and dictatorship of "King" James Jesse Strang.

On our way up that spring, we were delayed in the Straits of Mackinac by an ice gorge for about four days, and two of these days we lay at the dock at Mackinac Island. There, when we walked ashore off the dock, we left our first footprints in the sands of northern Michigan.

For many years previous to the time this story begins, the Government had maintained a garrison at Mackinac, and at the foot of the bluff, right under the very mouths of the cannon, stood the old John Jacob Astor House. This had been the headquarters and distribution station for the fur traders sent to the great north and west, as well as the point where the furs were assembled for shipment by the Hudson Bay Fur Company.

At the time of this story, and for many years afterward, the Astor House served the traveling public as a hotel, as well as being used for the business of the Hudson Bay Fur Company. As a child and young man, it sheltered and fed me for a day or two many times, and I enjoyed the stories of romance and adventure of some of those old Hudson Bay fur traders very much.

For about ten years I was intimately acquainted with three of them, and I have never known any other persons who had such a fund of interesting, first-hand adventures to recount as they did; and they would tell them in such an easy way that I think almost anyone would have believed them, whether they deserved it or not!

After we had enjoyed Mackinac for a couple of days, the ice moved and our boat proceeded to Beaver Harbor, where we landed late in April. We remained there three or four days.

After seeing the boats come in daily with their nets and fish, Father decided to buy an outfit and do fishing as well as coopering. He bought a good boat, the necessary nets and cordage, and cedar bark with which to roof a house, and loaded everything into the boat. With one hired man, who understood fishing and navigating a fish boat, we started for the head of the island, where we landed near the lighthouse. There we unloaded and pulled the boat up on the dry sand with blocks and tackle.

With the boat turned nearly bottom up, it made a very good shelter from the cold spring wind, after which Father and his man set about building a temporary habitation with pieces of lumber, poles and cedar bark, which we were able to occupy the next day. And there we left our first footprints in the sand as settlers in a new land.

Chapter 3
Father Becomes the Light Keeper

There are few restraining influences in a new country, and almost immediately after we settled on the sand near the lighthouse, my parents got acquainted with the Van Allen family and became very good friends.

Mr. Van Allen was the light keeper on Beaver Island, and he and Mrs. Van Allen were members of the Mormon Church. In those days the term "pseudo Mormon" was attached to all Mormons who rebelled at the unlawful and unchristian teaching and practices of their church, and this term would apply to the Van Allens.

They had been hoping for some means of escape from the Island, and with our arrival they thought they could see the way. As soon as Mr. Van Allen felt sure that he could safely do so, he came to Father with the request that Father take over the light until such time as the lighthouse tender should come, when, he felt sure, some satisfactory arrangement could be made. (This turned out to be Father's appointment as light keeper, which made us a fixture there, possibly for many years, if he should choose to keep it so long.)

Van Allen then arranged with some Indians to come on a certain night about midnight to spirit them away, which was accomplished without mishap.

You may think it strange that those pseudo Mormons should be obliged to steal away. You may think that all they would need to do would be to walk down on the dock and go aboard some steamboat.

But not only the Van Allens but other pseudo Mormons believed that if they should undertake to leave openly, that is, to quit the Mormon colony and Mormonism, they would not be permitted to leave the Island alive; and I think this belief was shared by the gentile fishing population of the region generally.

Friend Reader, as much as I dislike to record this feature of the situation here at this time, I feel that sooner or later it must be done, because to shirk it would be to betray my earlier promise to you to give you this little historical sketch as it occurred, without fear nor favor. The situation did not improve, but rather got worse, until it finally came to a head a few years later when "King" Strang was assassinated and the Mormon "kingdom" dispersed.

While our boat lay at the dock in Mackinac on our way up in the spring, we had spent much of the time ashore, going about from place to place, viewing the scenery and the natural beauty of the Island. We also got acquainted with the merchants and others and made a few purchases. Some of the merchants, with an eye to business, proposed to Father that they fit him out with a fishing rig, but as at that time he was not planning to fish, he did not buy.

We found the people to be a cleaver, sociable lot, inclined to be helpful as any resident people can be to strangers. What rather surprised Father was the fact that nearly every one with whom he conversed suggested to him that he should be armed if he was going to Beaver Island. Some went to some pains to make their suggestions impressive!

So finally he approached the Captain of the boat and inquired as to the conditions ahead of us, and was informed that all the gentile fishermen and coopers considered it necessary to be prepared to defend themselves in any emergency which might arise.

The guns with which the fishermen hereabout were armed were old Revolutionary and War of 1812 muskets, which would take a dozen buckshot for a charge. They were the old flintlock kind, with powder pan and flint, muzzle loaders—and were an ugly-looking thing to face. Well, when we left Mackinac, Father owned two of these big guns and a quantity of ammunition.

An event which occurred later that summer makes me think that Father was right to have procured his big guns, and I think it relieved him of any feeling of embarrassment on account of them. On one of the calls of the lighthouse tender, the Lieutenant inquired of Father if he was well armed, and on being informed of his possessions, he went to his room and brought out two beautiful shot guns. One was a little longer and heavier than the other, but either would chamber three buckshot.

As he gave them to Father, he said that perhaps Mrs. Smith would like the smaller one, and he made the rather significant remark that they might be found useful. He also included a supply of buckshot, bird shot, and caps. I think these were the first guns to use percussion caps my father had ever seen, as percussion caps had but recently been invented.

Taking charge of the light gave us a good dwelling for a home, as all the lighthouse towers and dwellings were of solid brick construction. But very little time and labor were required to care for the light, which left most of the time for Father to work at his trade. However, it was necessary for Father to keep two men, as that light had no assistant keeper in those days.

Keeping an extra man added that much strength to the little garrison, if occasion should arise where we might find ourselves placed on the defensive. It was thought that when it was generally known that there were three men and one woman (who could bring a hawk down out of a tall tree), all armed and behind brick walls, it would deter any ordinary marauding party from making an attack, and it probably did, for the only loss we suffered while we lived at the lighthouse was one gang of nets stolen out of the lake.

Keeping an extra man was also an advantage in that it left Father all his time for making barrels. This insured him a supply of barrels for his catch of fish, and that at first cost. A quantity of pine bolts for staves and heading was procured and the staves and heading were riven out so as to be seasoning. After this, they built quite a large, cheap building for shop, storage, net and fish house.

So, by the latter part of May, we seemed to be fairly well established, with only the daily routine work to be done.

Chapter 4
Our Year on Beaver Island

Very soon after the departure of the Van Allens, no less a personage than "King Strang" himself called at the lighthouse to inform Father of his plans. These were, briefly, to the effect that he, Strang, was going to place a Mormon in charge of the light unless our folks would join the Mormon Church, in which case Father would remain as keeper.

Father rather tersely informed Strang that no Mormon would be placed in charge of the light until such time as the Government should relieve him of any responsibility in the matter; as to joining the Mormon Church, that was not to be considered at all, and the question would admit of no further parley. He requested Strang to depart at once and without further comment, all of which was carried out.

James Jesse Strang was leader of a group of Mormons who were forced to leave Voree, Wisconsin, not by open violence but by being made to know that they were no longer wanted there. From Voree, they finally drifted to Beaver Island, some time about 1847 or 1848.

On Beaver Island, James Strang proclaimed himself Prophet and King. He seemed to hold state and federal laws in contempt, and arbitrarily made and enforced the laws for the local government. He was recognized as "King Strang" or "the Prophet James" by the Mormons, and was referred to as King Strang by the gentiles (as they called all non-Mormons).

At the time of their arrival on Beaver Island, Strang's followers were estimated to number twelve hundred or more, and at the time this story begins—1852—it was believed there were two thousand or more. By the fall of that year, all gentiles had been driven from the Island, abandoning homes and businesses.

There were quite a number of couples, both among the Mormons and among the gentiles, which consisted of a gentile husband and a Mormon wife. These families were very good people, and if they happened to be living among the Mormons they were always treated well by both Mormons and gentiles. But if they happened to live among the gentiles, they would get no favors during the periodical raids that were made on the fishermen, but suffered as the gentiles did.

However, when an investigation was being conducted by state or federal authorities, Strang would casually say, "Well, there is Mr. so and so, and Mr. Blank, and Mr. Blank Blank; these people are not Mormons and they have lived among us for some time. Perhaps they could tell you something of interest. It would do no harm to see them." And, of course, these people of their own knowledge would say nothing detrimental of either of the other parties or factions, and it is rather likely that whatever they did have to say would be more convincing than would the remarks of either other party. Yet these people were always under a shade of suspicion from both of the other factions.

Later in the season, Strang favored us with another call, but in some way he was made to understand that our folks were not receiving callers that day, and I think he must have been vexed, for he never came again.

The summer and fall passed quickly, as all were busy and interested in their work. Every day furnished a panoramic view of beautiful ships sailing past – ships of every conceivable rig, fore and aft and three mast schooners; barques, sloops, brigs and brigantines; besides the large steamers and coastwise traders and fishing boats. There were days when fifty large craft could be counted at one time, a veritable world in action, with all the changing scenes of sea and sky and light.

The winter settled down early, and we could no longer see the ships. That winter of 1852-1853 was a long and severe one -- the winter of the famine on the island, which was a subject for comment for many years afterward. Nearly all of the Mormons had gathered at the harbor for the winter, making too great a population for the housing capacity. What was to have been the last boat of the season failed to reach there, leaving them with almost no winter supplies. They were in desperate circumstances, and it was said that they survived only by living on the fish they were able to catch through the ice.

Our winter supplies had been ordered by an earlier boat and had reached us safely, so we had nothing to fear for ourselves that fall. Besides our food and clothing, two pairs of snowshoes and a supply of books and magazines had been laid in, also gilling twine, which would furnish some employment for the winter.

The fall before a family by the name of Hill, pseudo Mormons and nice people, had moved up to within about two miles of the lighthouse, and had remained there throughout the winter. With the aid of the snowshoes, friendly communication was kept up all during the winter. Father played the violin, so with all these things, and a boy, my folks were pretty well fixed!

It has always been a matter for conjecture as to what might have happened to us but for a seeming intervention of Providence when the ice broke up the next spring, and moved out so that boats could go up the island. Before any steamer had reached the island, three boats left the northern end of the island and made their way toward the head, carrying as many men as they comfortably could.

Before they reached our place, an Indian runner came to us and reported that they were coming to rob us, and we were entirely satisfied afterward that such had been their intention. But before they reached our place, a strong southerly wind drove in a large field of drift ice, so that they were unable to make a landing, thus making our position safe at least for the time being.

Chapter 5
Skille gul les, the Picnic and the Storm

In the spring of 1853, the Lieutenant from the lighthouse tender wanted to move my father to the light on Illeaux Galets, better known as Skille gul les. Jacob Burk, the present light keeper there, and his wife were getting old, and very much wanted to be relieved. So, in June, my parents consented to the move, and later that month the lighthouse tender took the family and such of our effects as our boat would not be able to carry at one load.

Reader, even the name itself is not as bad as the situation. About the only thing that can be said to its credit is that very little writing will suffice to describe it.

The island comprised about an acre of sand, with some rocks strewn around the shore. There was not even a blade of grass. On the north end, near the water's edge, was a poor, sickly little bunch of green osier, with no other vegetation. No part of the island was more than three feet above the lake level. The light tower and dwelling were about in the center, and the nearest land was the mainland, about five or six miles away.

I am sure Father was not aware of the conditions there, or he would never have gone, as neither fishing nor coopering could be carried on to any advantage.

There were no buildings, nor anything to make them of, and there was no timber for barrels. The trading schooners rarely touched there so these things could not be purchased conveniently. This was Skille gul les, where we made our footprints in the sand in yet another place! Words fail me to describe our lives there that summer and fall. I shall just have to leave it to your imagination!

My parents had not been to Mackinac since stopping there on our way up more than a year before, and we were beginning to need many things. The Burks, after being relieved, so they were free to leave whenever they chose, began to wonder whether it would be advisable for them to go back in the heat of summer to southern Pennsylvania. They had lived here several years in this cool climate, far out in Lake Michigan, where there was never any real heat, with nearly always a breeze—or a gale!

They finally decided to stay with us until the hot weather would be past for that year, so they offered to care for the light so we could make the trip to Mackinac. In those days, some lights were supplied with an assistant keeper and some were not. Skille gul les was, so we took the assistant with us.

By picking a day of favorable wind, the trip to Mackinac was made in one day. We stayed in Mackinac eight or nine days, trading, visiting and sightseeing. We bargained with Captain Kirkland to deliver our winter supplies in Little Traverse late in the fall, so they would be there when we arrived, after the close of navigation. Then, picking a favorable day for the return, the trip back to Skille gul les was made safely.

It finally turned out that the Burks stayed with us until October. My father's brother, more recently

known as Captain Timothy D. Smith, and another man came to the little island to make us a few days' visit. While they were with us, it was planned to go to the mainland to pick blackberries, as it was known there were great quantities of them, and it would make a fine picnic outing for a day.

So, one fine day we went, leaving the assistant with the light, as it was against the rules for all to leave the island at one time. When we arrived at the mainland, we all picked berries until noon, and then enjoyed a fine picnic dinner. After dinner, more berries were picked. But in the afternoon, it was noticed that the wind was rising and the weather was looking very threatening, and it was decided to start for the island at once.

The wind kept increasing, and when we were about a mile from the island, the jib had been taken in and the mainsail reefed. Then, with four men and two women, besides the usual ballast, all to windward, the strain on the foremast was great enough to carry away the "step" – a block of wood spiked to the keel into which the foot of the mast is stepped. As the mast careened over, it shoved or pried off the garboard streak – the streak of plank next to the keel – from the bow stem and the first timber back.

As soon as the foresail could be lowered and the spar righted, with the halyards carried to windward and well aft and made taut, the jib was on and with a reefed mainsail we could make some headway, but not very rapidly in that nasty sea.

During the time lost when the spar gave way, we had made some leeway, and now could not quite head on to the island. And as we could not now go about on the other "tack", things were looking pretty scary, with the wind rising steadily and the night getting close.

From the very first, it had taken one man working with might and main to stuff in and hold a quilt in such a way as to keep out part of the water. Even then, it took two men bailing, to keep the boat free enough to make much headway.

Well, of course, we made it or I would not be writing this story now! Running out in a northerly direction for some distance from the north end of the island was a reef. When we reached it, and were right over it, two men jumped overboard where the water was waist deep and towed the boat ashore. Someone may say in derision that God made that reef for our special benefit! Well, I thank Him for it, whether He had us in mind when He was making it or not, for it certainly served our purpose when we needed it!

Chapter 6
We Move to the Mainland

At the close of navigation that fall of 1853, we succeeded in making our way to Little Traverse on the mainland – the present day Harbor Springs. During the next eleven years we lived, and fished, and Father worked at his trade as a cooper in various areas – Middle Village and Cross Village to the north and Pine River and Yuba to the south. Then, in 1864, Father took up his homestead in Marion Township.

These were the years when most youngsters would be getting a formal education, but my attempts to do so were often met with frustration. It is true that the first summer in the lighthouse on Beaver Island, Mother began teaching me to read, and the next winter, when I was just four years old, she taught me to spell. Having almost no other way of passing my time, much more of it was spent with my lessons than the average little boy in school might spend.

I did have a few toys – a whole merchant marine of toy sail boats, once a dog for a short time, and yes, a cow! There was a big Mackinaw fish boat in which I could play when it was hauled up on shore on windy days. All of these things furnished some diversion, but mighty little formal education, though I believe they were a real help to me as they gave me much exercise and real enjoyment.

The next spring writing was added to my other lessons, and this was a decided help to me, as it required little teaching but lots of practice. Where the average school pupil gets only a few moments daily, or perhaps only two or three times a week, I spent hours daily practicing my writing skills.

Mother was an excellent teacher. I made good progress, as by the time I was six years old, I could read any book or paper with ease and fair understanding. My reading, spelling and writing ability were a surprise to all who visited us at the lighthouse. In these years, many strangers, whom I never saw but the one time, sent me books. One man sent me books for a number of years.

It was good that I had these auxiliary sources of learning because at the time we came to the region there were only about a half dozen children of school age, scattered along a coastline of more than two hundred miles, so an urgent need for schools had not yet arisen.

When schools did begin to appear, they were haphazardly operated, to say the least. They were carried on under the old rate bill system (or lack of system) and the school term ended whenever the teacher chose to remain away from school, which always occurred whenever the attendance became so small that the rate he or she could collect did not satisfy. And, if patrons of the school were not satisfied with the teacher, they just had to keep their children out of school, thus forcing the school to close. (They only had to pay for the days of actual attendance.)

And the teachers! There was no examination of teachers in those days, at least not in this country. Any young woman who had the temerity to say that she could teach school would be hired on just that recommendation. They could nearly all read easy words and could write their own names, and some could write more. One, whom I happened to go to longer than to any other during those years, did not reach the limit of her ability in mathematics until we finally got to long division. Then, of course, that was different!

In this connection, having mentioned the absence of schools, I will say that no one could feel the lack of a formal education more acutely or with deeper regret than I have all my life. My parents always regretted the circumstances that prevented my having at least a fair amount of schooling. Several times they moved quite long distances to some place where there was supposed to be a school, only to find that it was just about to close, or had already. Sometimes, I would get only about the last three or four days of the term.

There were no roads, and no need of them, when we had the broad expanse of Lake Michigan on which to travel by boat. We also had inland waterways, of which there were two separate chains of lakes and rivers, each nearly forty miles in length. Except for two portages, one of a mile or so and the other about four miles, this formed a continuous water route from Elk Rapids to Cheboygan.

The area embraced in the region I am dealing with is greater, I think, than that of some of our eastern states, and larger, I believe, than some of the nations of Europe. Naturally, there would be many settlements which would come into existence and make a more or less successful struggle for permanence.

With regard to the oldest settlements which I have already mentioned – Mackinac (first named Michilimackinac), Beaver Harbor, and Cross Village – I doubt if there is any way of knowing when these were first settled by white men, for it must have passed into the realm of conjecture or tradition some two or three hundred years ago.

Considering those which have survived in the order in which they were first settled, it seems fairly probable that Old Mission dates a little farther back than any of the others. The Presbyterian Board of Foreign Missions established a mission there with Reverend Peter Doughterty as missionary in 1839.

In 1847, Horace Boardman and a Mr. Gay settled at the head of Grand Traverse Bay, and soon after this two other families. This same year A.S. Wadsworth located at the mouth of a river which he named Elk River. From these beginnings came the Grand Traverse area (which included Yuba,) Traverse City and Elk Rapids.

The first white man to make the settlement at

Northport permanent (it was first called Wankazoo-ville) was George N. Smith, who began his missionary work to the Indians there in 1849 or 1850.

It is fairly probable that in the years 1850-1855, inclusive, New Mission, Suttons Bay, Benzonia, Glen Arbor, Bowers Harbor, Bear Creek and perhaps some others were established.

It was my privilege in my boyhood and young manhood to know these first settlers whom I have named (except one only) as well as hundreds of the real pioneers who came to this region, reaching from the Straits of Mackinac as far south as Frankfort, and to know the hardship and privation and suffering which was theirs to endure.

It is with difficulty that I attempt to restrain myself from devoting at least a little space to some of our little cities and towns as they exist today. I would like to describe Harbor Springs, the Little Traverse of my boyhood, circling as she does with her two summer resorts, two or three miles of the prettiest and best natural harbor to be found on the entire chain of Great Lakes, with that great bluff for a background – a beautiful sight as viewed from Little Traverse Bay.

I would like to tell you of little old Cross Village, her daring rivaling that of Quebec, perched as she is on the very brink of a bluff, perhaps one hundred and fifty feet above the level of Lake Michigan, with not a tree to break the force of the sweeping gale from the west and north.

I would like to tell you of Petoskey, the Bear River of this story, and of Norwood. Each is built on a rather steep sloping site from a very high background to the very water's edge, and each presents a breathtaking view from Lake Michigan, when the sun is well to the west.

And of course, I cannot pass without mentioning Charlevoix, the Pine River of my childhood and youth, the Charlevoix of my young manhood and older years. It is situated facing Lake Michigan on the west and Pine Lake on the east, with Round Lake, a sparkling basin of pure water in the very center of the city. The lakes are connected by the three shortest rivers anywhere, two of them being navigable for the largest fresh water ships.

Its scenery – its natural park with the bluff, its terraces with level tablelands on either side; its miles of paved streets and level driving roads; its summer resorts, beautiful cottages, and many summer hotels; its fishing, its fruits, its climate!

Oh, well, there is no stopping place, and as this story is not primarily about our modern cities and country but is about this region as a whole and about a time long past, I will return now and take up the narrative where I left off.

Chapter 7
Celebration at Cross Village

When we left the island in the fall of 1853 to settle at Little Traverse, we found quite a colony of fishermen and their families gathered there for the winter—probably a dozen families in all. While some were French, all were English speaking people. But as all were young married, or unmarried, I was still without English-speaking playmates.

Indian youngsters there were aplenty, and I spent most of my time with them. It was surprising, even to me, how readily I learned their language. While I probably didn't think of this at the time as increasing my education, it stood me in good stead a few years later in connection with the "third outstanding event" which I mentioned earlier.

The winter passed very pleasantly, and, with the opening of spring, the little colony scattered once more to their various points of interest. My folks decided to try the fishing at Pine River, so this spring of 1854 found us settled on the beach below the bluff, a little south of the mouth of the river. We were at the west end of the present natural park of Charlevoix—but, of course, there was no Charlevoix at that time.

A fisher family by the name of Hunter settled near us, and by the two crews helping each other, each family built a fairly good log house, with walls about six feet high and covered with cedar bark. When we left Pine River the latter part of June, these house walls were left standing, and no doubt were used by some one again. We used ours again when we returned to Pine River nearly two years later, in the spring of 1856.

So, once again, we made our footprints in the sand in a new place.

When we left Pine River in June, 1854, we went north, stopping at Little Traverse for a few days. Then we went on to Cross Village, where a house was rented, as we expected to stay until the next spring. Father then built quite a sizeable building for a shop and storage, where fishing and coopering were carried on as usual.

Another fisherman cooper by the name of Stoddard settled here about the time we did. He arranged with Father for berth room in the shop, so there were two coopers, each making fifty barrels a week, which was more than they needed for their own catch of fish. This was inducement to other fishermen to settle here, and by the last of July there were seven or eight boats, which made up a colony of about twenty five men, including four coopers, and about fifteen or more women—a pretty strong colony in case of attack.

Where several boats were huddled together, one of them could always be spared for a trip to Mackinac for supplies. Generally on these trips some one of the fishermen would go with his boat and his wife with him, and they would buy and bring back supplies for all the others. He would leave his two men home to do his work, and take one from some other crew with him. The other boats would set and lift his nets, and his two men would do all his other work. To have three men gone for a week or so would make rather hard work for the others, but no one seemed too concerned over that.

During the fall of 1854 and the spring of 1855, it was noised about that there were to be Fourth of July celebrations and regattas, not only at Mackinac, where they had been held for several years, but also at some place on the west shore and another on the east shore of Lake Michigan. During the spring it was decided to hold the one on the east shore at Cross Village. As we were already there, my parents decided to stay until after the Fourth of July.

There was an underlying objective in holding these get-together celebrations that was not advertised, but was generally understood by the fishermen. The Mormon depredations were getting to be unbearable, and it was thought that the situation could be discussed at these celebrations to see if some means could be devised or plans formulated that would stop the thieving, burning and murdering that was being carried on.

Beaver Island in those days was the base of operation of one of the most destructive nests of pirates the world had ever harbored. Small vessels, carrying a crew of two, three or four men, were disappearing and leaving no trace of their ever having existed. It was said that some large vessels had disappeared just as mysteriously, and some boats were being stolen.

Cooper shops and fish houses were being burned; nets and fish were being stolen out of the water and from houses. A few individual fishermen had dropped out of sight as effectually as if the earth had opened and swallowed them up. The fishermen felt strongly that it was time some check was put on this lawlessness and crime.

As the time drew near for the celebration to begin at Cross Village, the boats began to appear, some of them arriving as much as a week before the Fourth of July. By July 3rd, there must have been between fifty and sixty boats, and a veritable village of tents.

At sunrise on the Fourth of July, a salute was fired and the good time was on! There must have been more than one hundred men and nearly a hundred women, and they certainly had as good a time as any carefree group of good people could possibly have. During the day, those old army flintlocks made noise enough to satisfy the average small boy of today!

A vacant store building in the village had been rented and was used for a dining hall for the mid-day dinner and for meetings and dancing at night.

Every mid-day dinner was a free-for-all feast! There were boxes and barrels and bags and bales of all manner of food and drinks that could be found anywhere. One gang of nets was set and one lifted each day to provide fresh fish, and a fat pig supplied fresh pork. Rabbits and partridges furnished at least one dinner, and wild pigeons could be had any morning. The entire supply of milk from several cows was made available and, well, there was nothing lacking.

Each unit supplied its own breakfast and supper at the tent. There were games and boating each forenoon and music, singing, and dancing every evening. I feel quite sure that during that festive season the plotting and lovemaking was begun that culminated in several weddings that fall!

The afternoons were devoted to the Mormon matter, and it was plainly evident from the very first that the law-and-order element was very much in the majority. It was decided to make a strong appeal to the State of Michigan for protection; and if the State could not, or would not, do something toward bettering conditions within a year, there would be another assembling the next Fourth of July, when the matter of self protection and how to go about it would be considered.

I suppose that what I have written about the celebration at Cross Village would apply almost exactly to the other celebrations in the area that year.

Chapter 8
Who Were Those Fishermen?

After about three weeks of a most enjoyable time at Cross Village that summer of 1855, the fishermen broke camp and went their several ways to begin preparation for the fall fishing. Before their sails fade into the horizon, I would like to say a few words about who they were and what they accomplished.

Reports written in later years, especially after their encounters with the Mormons, sometimes presented these fishermen as a group of ignorant, malicious and lawless ruffians. But I can assure you from my own experience that they were not heathen. For the most part, they were a good, clean, self-respecting, law-abiding, hospitable, enterprising lot.

A few years prior to the beginning of this story, news of this country began to attract the attention of many ambitious young men, who began coming, just a few at first but more each succeeding year. By 1852, there were about three hundred boats fishing in this area of Lake Michigan.

Some of these young men probably came from the sheer love of adventure, but most of them came with the hope of making themselves better off. Nearly all went back home that first fall, but all came again the next spring, generally bringing a friend or two with them. Many brought a young wife, and perhaps her sister or friend.

As I have said before, Beaver Harbor was becoming a center of great importance to this region. The harbor itself was a safe refuge in any storm and furnished shelter for thousands of ships of every size and rig.

The fishing population grew and spread up the shores, on the mainland where Frankfort is now, and to the islands as far south as the Manitou Islands. Soon South Manitou with its beautiful harbor attracted many fishermen, and a good steamboat dock was built. It became a community center and an enterprising shipping point.

Also, the cutting and hauling of wood for the steamboats made work through the winter for all who cared to work, for at that time and for many years afterward all steamboats used wood for making steam. Coal was not much in use at that time so very little was carried west. As late as 1874 I rode on a western train hauled by a locomotive burning wood.

Think of the people who first settled America. Even after acquiring the land, they needed buildings, farm tools and equipment, all kinds of live stock, seeds, fencing, forges, roads, bridges, boats and ships, schools, churches, libraries, mills and factories, with mechanics of all trades, doctors, lawyers, teachers and preachers.

Then they had to work and wait many weary months—sometimes a whole year—before they could realize as much as a hill of corn or potatoes on this labor and investment. For two hundred years, the millions of pioneers who pushed further and further west repeated these experiences of want, privation and suffering. The pioneer in a new country has always had a hard time, except in one instance, that of which I am writing.

The pioneer fishermen came here not to clear the land and build, plant and sow, nor to suffer from disease and privation. They came here to harvest the crop which a kind Providence had been growing and ripening since the day when Noah started on his cruise looking for land—a crop already to his hand which it seemed could never be exhausted.

The equipment was very simple and relatively inexpensive. It consisted of a good Mackinaw boat, which would last eight years or more, and anywhere from twenty to forty gill nets and the necessary cordage. The whole cost between two hundred and fifty and four hundred dollars, and any man who was not known to be dishonest could get the necessary outfit on credit. Many such a rig has caught fish enough to pay for itself in ten days when the fish were on the shoals late in the fall.

I do not wish to convey the impression that this fishing business was not work, for it was very real work. But it was no such work as ridding the land of a heavy growth of timber, and then for years working among and finally disposing of the stumps and stones. It was not like the days in the haying and harvest field, nor like digging potatoes, nor like cutting and shocking corn, nor like harrowing all day on the soft ground, where one's feet and legs would ache with fatigue. It was more like the winter choring on a farm, where there may be more than a dozen light jobs each day, with a little space between any job and the next one.

The young men of this country soon learned that they not only could support wives in the fishing industry, but that they could support them as well as the rich people could back home, and could get ahead in the world as well.

True, for one or two years they went back in the fall to the old home. Then the husband would think that he could not afford to waste the next winter while there was so much necessary work to be done. There were new nets to be knitted, the used ones to be mended, floats and buoys to be made, sinker and anchor stone to be prepared, the boat to be re-caulked and painted, and barrel timber to be gotten out.

He felt his wife had better go home, but then he would get to wondering how he would ever get through that long winter without that wonderful baby of theirs. But he guessed he would get through somehow! Besides, it was not fair to the old folks to keep Mary and little Charlie away from them for such a long time.

Well, of course, she was reluctant to go and leave him to "bach" it all winter. But then her heart would swell with the pride of a young mother who would soon lay her first baby in her dear old mother's arms, and listen to the praises of Grandma and Grandpa. So, yes, she would go—but she would hurry back in the spring!

Why should these stalwart young fishermen and their handsome young wives and the unmarried young men and women, most of whom had spent one or more seasons here and had escaped the fall before with their lives—why should they be so eager to get back here, to get back to God's country? The stories of suffering and privation, to be endured in the "awful country" no longer held any terrors for these people. They crowded the first boats up each spring to capacity, slept on couches, on the cabin floor, and even on deck in their hurry to get back.

The experience of my own parents was typical. The first year they came, there was a settled resolution on their part to return home in time for the holidays, and to spend the winter in the old home town. They even thought it probable that they might be satisfied to settle down there permanently.

Especially during the winter of 1857 and 1858, Father and Mother often discussed the question of returning to Detroit to engage in some kind of business. In the six years they had been here, enough had been saved to make a fair start in a business or to buy a good farm back in Redford, the old home town.

But, as spring came, the lure of God's great country proved too strong, and they would decide to wait until the next fall. And this thing of putting it off from spring until fall and from fall until spring became a fixed habit, until it was more than thirty years before they saw the old home place again, and then it was only for a two weeks' visit.

Chapter 9
A Sense of Impending Danger

If you remember, when I made this digression, we were at Cross Village and it was July, 1855. In the spring of that year an election had been held, which may have been the first election ever held there. Father was elected Justice of the Peace, which strangely enough will have to do with the very first event in the next year. This, in turn, will have to do with establishing the date of one of the important events of that year, 1856, which, as far as I know, has been given a wrong date by all who have written about it. This will be taken up and made clear later.

In the fall of 1854, some vessel had lost a deck load of lumber, which had drifted ashore north of Middle Village and along the shore for a mile or so. This had been salvaged by the Indians, and since they had no use for it, it could be bought very cheap.

So, at the close of the Fourth of July celebration festivities at Cross Village, Father went to Middle Village, which was sixteen miles north of Little Traverse. He bought a quantity of lumber sufficient for a good set of buildings, and he and his men built an excellent house, into which we moved early in August. Then a fish house and quite a large shop, with room enough for two berths and storage for about three hundred barrels, were built.

A quantity of seasoned barrel stuff, together

with Father's whole fishing outfit, were still at Cross Village, so they were then moved to the new location a mile north of Middle Village. And again, we were making footprints in the sand in a new place!

During the spring and summer of 1855, the Board of Foreign Missions (the name was changed later to Home Missions) had acquired some land about half a mile back from Middle Village. They had also bought some of the salvaged lumber from the Indians, had built a good school house and dwelling, and had sent Gardner Turner here as Missionary.

Mrs. Turner came with him, so we had a white family (with no children) for neighbors, only a mile from us. They were from Cincinnati, and arrived here just about the time we did. Later that fall, a family by the name of Johnson settled here also, consisting of Mr. and Mrs. Johnson and three daughters. Two of the daughters were young women, and the youngest was about a year older than I, and she was the first white playmate I ever had.

The Middle Village fishing grounds, where we established ourselves that summer of 1855, proved to be one of the best fishing grounds in this part of the lake. I think Father must have made a net profit of approximately a thousand dollars that fall. It had been his best year since being engaged in the fishing business and it seemed that we were established for some time to come. But when two or three lifts had been made and there were several barrels of fish in the fish house, a raid was made on us one night and all the nets, cordage, and such other things as they could take were stolen. This included the fish, except for two or three barrels which they could not take with them.

Then fire was set in the shop and fish house, and in the morning all we had left was the boat, the two or three gangs of nets which were in the lake, and the new nets which had not been seamed and happened to be in the men's shanty. (Father had expected to finish them a little later and use them for the late fishing.) Two kits of coopers' tools and about fifty barrels had burned in the shop. The marauders had carried a big armful of shavings from the shop and had thrown them into the boat, probably intending to burn it, but for some reason they didn't. I think the total loss must have been about four hundred dollars.

The day after this raid on us, Father and the men agreed on a plan by which they could operate the fishing rig on shares. Father was to furnish the boat, the twenty new nets, and the two or three gangs that were in the lake, as well as the barrels in which to pack the fish they would catch. He would help with any work that would be necessary to do at night, and the men would seam the new nets, make the floats and buoys, and help to build a shop and fish house. At the close of the season, Father was to have half, and the men half of the intake, which turned out to be a very satisfactory deal to all concerned.

Determined to lose no time after arriving at this agreement, Father and the men started for Little Traverse that same evening. Father had to get a kit of coopers' tools and such other items as would be needed to complete the equipment. Father also had to buy supplies for the family, and the men were to supply themselves with anything they might need during the fall.

Over at Little Traverse, a man named Richard Cooper had established a store, the first store there, and had completed a dock at which steamboats could land for wood and from which he could ship the fish which he expected to deal in from that time on. As the time drew near that we fisher folk would be scattering to the various fishing grounds, Mr. and Mrs. Cooper invited us to a six o'clock supper, an old time feast followed by a dance.

Just as we were about to sit down at the tables, in came Mrs. John S. Dixon from Pine River, looking—well, I simply cannot describe her appearance— and in a moment she collapsed into unconsciousness. Instantly all was excitement and confusion and some thought she was dying. But the women began doing whatever they could, rubbing and using such restoratives as were at hand, and in a little time she began to return to consciousness.

When she had recovered sufficiently to be questioned, she said she had left her home at Pine River just after two o'clock that afternoon (which was verified later by some of the people at Pine River), that she had gone north to the lake and had followed the beach from there to Little Traverse. She said that there were places where the fallen timber reached into the water, and that she could wade around quicker than she could crawl through the thick tops. When she reached us, she was wet from her neck down.

A few days before this, Mr. Dixon was obliged to leave home to be gone three or four weeks and had left her alone. On the day before she made this sprint, a vessel had come from Beaver Island to Pine River, having on board several Mormons beside the crew. On arriving at Pine River, the Mormons went to the Dixon place, remained about for some time, and then hanged Dixon in effigy, which frightened Mrs. Dixon very much. [Editor's Note: A replica of Dixon was hanged.]

The following morning, the day of her flight, they returned and took the oxen and the two cows away with them. This added to her fear until she was beside herself with fright. By early afternoon, being unable to endure the torture of fear any longer, she fled, with the results as I have given above.

When navigation closed that fall, we were supplied with everything we should need for the winter. From the settling in of winter until well into February, about twenty nets were knitted. Everything was in readiness for the new season's work.

At the close of this season of 1855, two of Father's brothers decided to spend the winter with us. On January 14 of the new year, his brother, Timothy D. Smith, and Miss Ellen M. Johnson, were married at our house by my father as Justice of the Peace. Mrs. Smith resided in Charlevoix for nearly fifty years afterward, and still had her marriage certificate, written out on that occasion and dated January 14, 1856.

On February 18, 1856, a daughter was born to my parents, and I began looking forward with impatience to the time when I should have a little sister for a playmate.

During this winter, unforeseen changes were in the making. Several of the Little Traverse acquaintances got ponies and drove to our place to try to induce Father to change his plans for the next spring. They had decided to go to Pine River for the spring fishing, and they wanted very much for our folks to join the group there, not only to strengthen the colony by that much but, I feel sure, they were considerably worried for our safety since we were alone. After much persuasion, my parents decided to join forces with the Pine River group.

So, when the ice left the shore that spring, with everything in readiness, the boat was sent with a barrel or two of salt, some fish barrels, the bark to roof the house body we had left there two years before, and two gangs of nets. They were to set these nets when crossing Little Traverse Bay.

The other things were to be left in the house, and they were to return for the family. The day we moved, another gang of nets was set, and the following day, still another and the first two gangs were lifted. The boat limped in with all she could carry, so the season's fishing was well underway!

The Little Traverse contingent was three or four days late reaching here because the ice in Little Traverse Bay moved out later than usual, but when they had all arrived, there were eight or nine boats fishing out of Pine River. Later, our boat had to be sent back to Middle Village for a load of staves and heading, so all were busy.

But everybody was restless, with a sense of impending danger, or of some unseen trouble threatening. Reports of marauding parties and their depredations were being heard almost daily. The Indians—the best spies in the world—were constantly reporting something that had been or was about to be done, and they were rarely mistaken.

By the middle of May, the very air seemed charged with imminent danger, and the fishermen were talking of taking their nets out of the water. And yet, there seemed to be no real reason for doing so, until one night, several Indians came in a boat from Garden Island and warned the group of fishermen that the Mormons had decided to make an attack on us very soon, with forces enough to annihilate the little colony.

Chapter 10
Battle of Pine River

From the time the Indians brought us the warn-
ing of the possibility of a Mormon attack, there was a
night watch, in which two men patrolled the beach to a
point some distance to the southwest of where we lived,
ours being the last house of the group. The boats began
bringing the nets ashore, thoroughly drying nets and
cordage and arranging everything for a quick move.
However, no move could be made until such time as
some trader should come along to buy the fish and un-
used barrels and extra barrels of salt.

This "watchful waiting" time was used planning and talking over what would be best to do. Some
thought it best to join some other colony, thus building
up strength to withstand an attack. Others thought that
to do so would work to the advantage of the invaders,
as they could easily organize an overwhelming force,
while if we scattered only a few would suffer from an
attack at any one time. But as no move could be made
yet, it was left to decide when or if the time came to do
so.

As to the strength of the colony, there were nine
boats fishing here at that time and two, perhaps three,
coopers. There must have been about twenty six or
twenty eight men, and fifteen to eighteen women, some
of whom could handle a musket with telling effect.

My father's brother, Captain Timothy D. Smith, was at that time fishing somewhere on the north shore. Not knowing whether we were aware of the impending attack on us—also not wishing to lose a reasonable share in any unusual excitement—he left his young wife alone, with the nearest family several miles away, and came to our assistance with his two men.

He was here but a day or two when one morning three boats were seen out on the lake approaching this landing. The wind was light and they were coming slowly, and as they came nearer it was plainly evident that they were carrying as many men as they comfortably could. Since it was thought that this must be the Mormon attacking party, there was considerable anxiety on the part of the fishermen, and it is safe to say that every gun was examined and every preparation made to give them a warm reception!

To have this affair clearly understood, a little descriptive matter concerning the natural conditions at that time seems desirable. At the foot of the bluff, in what is now the natural park facing Lake Michigan in Charlevoix, there was at that time a narrow ravine only a few feet in width and five feet or so in depth, and between it and the lake there was a low ridge of sand dunes.

This little ravine can yet be seen in places, and in other places it has been filled in by drifting sand. But at that time a person could pass along the foot of the bluff without being seen from the lake to a point back of and very close to the Savage home (which was the house nearest to the mouth of the river) and there be hidden from view by a sand knoll. Having explained this much, I think you will be able to visualize this affair just about as it was carried out.

One of my father's men was named John Going, a capable, strong, happy-go-lucky daredevil, redheaded and a stutterer. The other man was Lewis Gebeau, a capable, reliable, likeable man, who was a resident of Charlevoix for many years. (Nearly forty years after this event about which I am writing, he lost his life with all on board the ill-fated steamship Vernon, when she foundered in a terrific gale on Lake Michigan some twelve or fifteen miles off Two River Point.)

Mrs. Savage had invited all the women to her house for a quilting bee that day, so the neighbor women were at the Savage home. It appeared that the Mormons were going to make their landing in front of there, so the fishermen rushed down that ravine and up behind that last sand dune to within four or five rods of the Savage house without having been seen by the Mormons. They reached there just about the time the Mormons were landing.

Gebeau and Going had each carried three guns, and Father had carried me on his back. When the halt was made back of Savage's, Father asked Gebeau to care for me so that he would be free to rush to Mother's assistance if that should seem necessary. Gebeau told me to take hold of his trouser leg and to hang on— which of course I did!

When the Mormons landed they pulled their boats up and just enough so that they wouldn't drift away and walked quite leisurely up to the house. The women hadn't noticed their approach until they were landing, and then shut and locked the door. I think some of them were pretty badly frightened. When the Mormons had pounded on the door until it seemed it might be broken in, some woman unlocked it and faced the crowd outside.

Then one of the Pierce Brothers began telling the women that they (the Mormons) "were going to wade in their husbands' blood up to their knees before they should leave here". When he had delivered himself of that much of his story, it seemed to have had a powerful effect on John Going. He swung his musket to his shoulder at once and whanged away, and at the same time triggered his automatic stutterer, and between his unearthly noises and the buckshot, which was taking immediate effect, the invaders were completely surprised and staggered, and the battle was on.

As soon as the Mormons could fairly take in the situation, and the disadvantage they were at from being exposed, they made a run for their boats. While getting shoved off and under way they were treated to more buckshot, and several of them had to be helped into the boats.

As they were leaving the shore, the fishermen made a dash for the house, and while we were exposed in the open, the Mormons fired several shots, one of which caught Gebeau and went through the thick of his leg below the knee, the very leg that I was holding onto! But it so happened that he was the only one of the fishermen injured.

There were no Mormons killed, but several were wounded, some quite severely. In making their way back to the Island, some of them fell in with the Barque Morgan and requested the Captain to take them on board, which he did, but most of them took to their own boats and went on to the Island.

Two or three days after this skirmish, Captain Kirkland came with his schooner and bought everything there was to spare, and our little colony dispersed, each family going where it thought best.

When we left Pine River near the middle of June, we went to Little Traverse, where my parents rented a house and a building for a shop and Father went to work at his trade. We had been there only two or three days when the news came that King Strang had been shot and killed. It turned out that he was not killed, but fatally wounded, and was removed to his former home and his lawful wife in Wisconsin, where he died a couple of weeks (or one account says nineteen days) later.

Not only is the assassination of King Strang an established date, which occurred, as I remember it, shortly after this skirmish, which has since been called the Battle of Pine River. But there are two other established dates which I mentioned earlier which also place the battle as occurring in 1856, instead of 1853 which other accounts have given.

One is the date of Timothy and Ellen Smith's marriage on January 14, 1856. You can decide for yourself whether her being left alone on that lonesome beach, miles from another person, would make a strong and lasting impression on her mind of the fact that her husband was away at Pine River, where it was expected there would be trouble which might be so serious as to leave her a widow.

The second date is February 18, 1856, when my sister, Ida, was born. Can I ever forget that this precious baby sister, then only a few months old and so small that she could only sit bolstered up with pillows in her cradle, was in peril on that fateful day when the Mormons came ashore at Pine River?

Do you think that I, surrounded and submerged in primitive nature, with only a few adults for associates, hearing and seeing their plans and preparations for defense of their lives and property against a conscienceless foe—could I fail to know what was taking place?

Reader, just as your little boy learned the multiplication table by studying it, repeating it over and over until it became so fixed in his memory that he could never forget it, so I lived over and over the same tragic experiences of those days and, all unknown to myself at the time, committed them indelibly to memory.

Chapter 11
Mormons Leave, Settlers Return

With the death of King Strang, the Mormons became utterly demoralized and disorganized. There was no man among them who was strong enough as a leader to fill Strang's place. Besides the piracies on the gentile population, the stronger ones preyed on the weaker. Stores and public property were plundered. Chaos, crime and confusion reigned.

The fishermen believed that while the Mormons were without a capable leader and master they could be routed and driven out of the country. So a call was sent out to all the fishermen about this part of the lake to meet at Beaver Harbor at a certain date, and to come prepared to rid this region of the Mormons for all time. At the appointed time the fishermen, nearly the whole gentile population, and some Indians were assembled at the harbor, and the Mormons were ordered to leave at once. I think that in three or four days there were no Mormons left in this part of the state.

They were not permitted to take anything with them except just what would suffice for their immediate needs. There was, no doubt, something of a scramble among the gentiles to possess themselves of the abandoned Mormon property. Before the last of the Mormons were off the island, some found themselves occupying very good houses, all furnished.

Farms, stock, implements, cattle, horses, houses, goods, furniture, docks, boats, lumber—everything, in fact, that a couple thousand "free booters" had accumulated in nine or ten years—became free plunder. Possession was recognized as ownership, and I never heard of a single instance of trouble or dispute over anything. Each one simply kept whatever he wanted, if he could get it first!

By nature my father was not vindictive, and I am glad in this connection to be able to say truthfully that he had no part in the turbulence and turmoil of that time, nor did he ever plan, nor in any way help, to bring about disorder or crime. Nor did he in any way benefit by the discomfort of the Mormons, except as all benefited by having a serious menace removed.

Although he suffered considerable property loss at different times, losses for which it was generally believed they were responsible, the only time in all these years that he did—or at least may have done—any of them any harm was at the Battle of Pine River, which I have already described.

For two years out of our first five in this country, we were in Government lighthouses, which was almost equivalent to a guarantee of immunity from their lawlessness, although we did have a certain amount of harassment. But to commit lawless depredations on or to Government property, or the keeper, would have been a rather serious charge to meet. The Mormons knew this, so it is fairly probable that the other fishermen generally suffered more than we did.

So now, friend Reader, this story, so far as it has to do with the Mormons, is drawing to a close. But I wish to add, in a spirit of fairness and with a feeling of friendliness and respect for all decent people, that among the Beaver Island Mormons there were some good, law-abiding, Christian people. These people had no part in the criminal practices carried on by the evil element, which unfortunately, however, was greatly in the majority.

Almost without exception this better element were pseudo-Mormons, and would gladly have left everything they had in the world if only they could escape from the Island with their lives, and a few succeeded in doing so.

The two men who shot and killed James Jesse Strang, the Mormon King and Prophet, or at least attempted to kill him, made no effort to escape, but went on board the government ship and gave themselves up to the law. After they were taken to Mackinac, turned over to the sheriff, and put in jail, the citizens of Mackinac opened the jail and gave them their freedom, and they were never indicted and brought to trial.

It seems fairly obvious that the reason the Mormons were ousted from the several places where they established themselves over the years, there to carry on their nefarious practices, was that a point always came where forbearance and endurance had reached their limit, and the non-Mormon people were compelled to take the law into their own hands or themselves be destroyed.

As you may remember, some two or three years before, John S. Dixon had come into possession of a tract of land at Pine River, and in 1855 had settled there with his family with the intention of developing his land, but the attitude of the Mormons was so threatening and so harassing that he was obliged to leave.

But this summer of 1856, after the Mormon situation had finally been settled, the Dixon family had returned, determined that this time they would not be driven away. They began at once to clear and improve the land and to erect good log buildings, and they had brought with them some livestock. In making these beginnings, he was the first white man to start a real farm between Elk Rapids and the Straits of Mackinac.

Later this same summer John Miller and family settled on the shores of Pine Lake where Boyne City now is, Medad Thompson and family near what is now the electric power plant in Charlevoix, and Samuel Horton and family at what is locally known as Horton's Bay.

Besides these four families—Dixon, Miller, Thompson and Horton—who became permanent settlers in that summer of 1856, there were seven or eight other families, who as transients left for other parts that fall. Among the latter, two or three families were Mormons.

With the Hortons came Archibald Buttars, a young single man, who left later for Elk Rapids, Grand Traverse, and Northport. He came back in 1869 to what had formerly been Pine River, which had by then come to be known as Charlevoix, and lived there many years thereafter.

The above four families are all that I can recall as having remained in Pine River that winter of 1856-1857. None of them were Mormons, and all expected to open up and develop farms, and all did so and all grew old and finally finished their lives on these farms.

Chapter 12
Treaty with the Indians

The house in Little Traverse, to which we moved in June, 1856 stood on the northwest corner of a plot of land of an acre or more, at what was then the extreme east end of the main, and almost the only, street in the village. At the west end, the street ended abruptly in front of the Catholic Church, the church standing in such a way that the street could go no further.

This plot of land on which we were living had been planted to apple trees many years previous to this time, and those old apple trees furnished beautiful shade. The Indian boys and I spent a great deal of our time there with our bows and arrows.

Shortly after we moved there the federal Government sent agents to treat with the Indians for their rights to a considerable tract of land reaching, I think, from somewhere near what is now the line between Charlevoix and Antrim Counties, north to the Straits of Mackinac, and from Lake Michigan on the west nearly across the state on the east.

The Council, as it was called, was held in the shade of this old apple orchard, right where we were living, and I, having nothing else in particular to do, attended these sessions every day.

In eight or nine days an agreement was arrived at between the Government agents and the Indian

Chiefs and head men, and by the terms of this agreement the Indians became wards of the Government. They were to be protected in all their rights and privileges, and were to be cared for and assisted in many ways, all tending towards a reasonable civilization.

By the terms of this agreement any Indian, male or female, twenty one years of age or older, might select for himself or herself a tract of land not to exceed forty acres; and as the younger ones became of age, for a period of, I think, seven years from the date of this contract, they too might make such selection. The land was to become the property of each individual without cost to them.

It was also specified that the Government should pay to every Indian living on pay day, without regard to age or sex—simply those alive on that day—twenty dollars in gold each year for a period of five years. Then the amount would be reduced to fifteen dollars a year for the next five years, then ten dollars a year for the next ten years, and then to cease. The first payment was to be made that fall.

In addition to the gold, the heads of families were to receive some other things—blankets, clothing, guns, as well as live stock, including horses and cattle. The Government was to furnish them a blacksmith and a farmer—a man to teach them how to farm. Beginning with the next year, the Government was to build school houses and maintain schools.

As I remember it, it was also proposed that at the expiration of this twenty-year period, during which they would be drawing their annuities, if they should have made reasonable progress towards civilization they were to become citizens.

But then a new and unexpected condition arose.

The Indians were not, and never had been, citizens of this or any other government, and later the Government admitted that they could not be drafted for soldiers in our Civil War because they were not citizens. But in spite of this, at the next election the adult males claimed the right to vote, and continue to exercise this right at all subsequent elections.

It was a strange circumstance. There appeared to be no precedent to govern in the matter. I think it was a Detroit lawyer who took the matter up on behalf of the Indians and argued the case somewhat as follows: that the Indians had never been citizens of any government; that they were the last of a race that had always lived here; that they had rights which had always been recognized by the Government; that the Government had treated with them, and had bargained with them as if they were capable of making and carrying out their part of agreements, and was already paying them for their former rights to a property of great value; that they bought, sold, and owned real estate and other property in their own individual right, and that the titles they gave were considered valid; that their property was assessed and they paid taxes the same as other individuals.

But opinion was divided, and it remained a question for debate for many years, in fact until President Lincoln's Emancipation Proclamation, when it no longer seemed worth discussing.

The man who acted as Government interpreter at this treaty or council was Robert Rodd, who a little later translated the New Testament Gospels and the hymns in use at that time by the Presbyterian Church, into the Indian language. I presume this Robert Rodd might have been a relative of Daniel Rodd, who acted as government interpreter at Old Mission in 1850.

You possibly noted that the payments to the Indians were to be made in gold. For many years prior to the time of this story and for about two years after—1860 and 1861—the money in circulation was gold and silver but in rather limited amounts.

In addition, there was a large volume of bank bills which were always insecure and were called "wildcat money". One of those bills might be worth its face one day and be worthless the next. So in passing that money it was customary for the person paying it out to write his name on the back of the bill, and sometimes the date, right to the hour. Then if it could be shown afterward that it was spurious at the time he passed it, he would have to redeem it with good money.

In any deal that was being negotiated the seller would generally ask "What kind of money?" and if it was gold or silver the deal went through; but if it was "wildcat money" he might refuse to take it and the deal would be off. It was optional with both the seller and the buyer—the first whether he would take paper and the latter whether he could pay in specie or not.

Early during the Civil War the Government issued "greenbacks" and "fractional currency" and made them legal tender for all ordinary business. The "wildcat" bills were collected and sent in to the banks for redemption, which finally disposed of them.

Soon after this council with the Indians took place, in the summer of 1856, our family moved back to Middle Village, which we had left early the spring before to join the group at Pine River. As you have probably guessed, my part in the Battle of Pine River was the second "outstanding event" of my life, which I mentioned earlier.

Why we did not go immediately to Middle Village after that battle scattered the little colony so completely is unclear. You will remember that we had a house and several other buildings there and had established a good fishing business.

There were in Little Traverse that summer Richard Moses Cooper, Myron Geer, John Papinaw, Harrison Miller, Joseph Payant, Joseph Graverat, Joseph Gilbo, Joseph McGulpin, my father Thomas Smith, and one other whose name I cannot recall, all with their families. Besides this, there were more than a dozen young single men and nearly that many young single women. Perhaps we all felt safer if we stayed close together.

But the fact that Father chose to spend a few weeks first in Little Traverse turned out very well as far as I was concerned. That was in connection with the third "outstanding event"—my part that fall in the distribution of their annuities to some of the Indians of the region. The fact that I was able to "sit in" on those conferences under the apple trees was, no doubt, a good background in preparation for that event, about which I shall tell you later.

Chapter 13
Dangerous Mission to Indian Friends

The last thing for me to record as having occurred in this eventful year of 1856 was the carrying
out of the Government's treaty obligation to the Indians. This took place, as I remember it, the last week in
October, and was of unusual interest to the people of
this region.

The Indians were looking forward with keen an-
ticipation to the time when each would receive twenty
dollars in gold, with which to supply themselves with
such things as they would need for the winter. And the
whites—or at least some of them, I am sorry to say—
were looking forward to a rich harvest of gold dollars!

By the time the paymaster reached Little Traverse there must have been between eight and a dozen
small schooners anchored in the harbor, each having
on board a small stock of provisions, and a big stock
of bad whiskey and low grade moral character. By the
night of the first day of the payments, it was pretty wild
around Little Traverse, and this continued for a week
thereafter.

As we were living at the Middle Village fishing
grounds at that time, about sixteen miles from Little
Traverse, we escaped most of the turmoil and rowdy-
ism and horror of the days and nights following this
payment time. In the course of a week or ten days the

Indians of our vicinity began drifting back home, most of them worse off than they were before receiving their twenty dollars.

Some of the traders must have found veins of gold that turned dollars into their pockets faster than any forty-niner ever did in California! There is not the shadow of a doubt that hundreds of the Indians, including many of the women, were dead drunk and robbed of their gold by some of the traders within a few hours of the time they received it.

In nearly all villages and community centers, there were some very old people, some sick, some very young, and some having other reasons why they could not go on long journeys at a certain time, and perhaps not at all. So as payment time drew near, the Indians in Middle and Cross Villages, who would not be able to go to Little Traverse to get the twenty dollars due them, became very anxious.

Several of the Indians came to Father for counsel as to what could be done. Some wanted him to go to the paymaster to intercede for them and vouch for them. Some wanted him to write to the paymaster on their behalf, or to assist them in some way to get their money. But Father felt the paymaster might be too busy to pay attention either to him or to his letters.

On thinking the matter over, and without saying anything to me about it, he suggested to the Indians that they get me to go with them, as I could speak the Indian language better than any other white person, and as I knew their aged and sick and their circumstances better than anyone else. (Remember that I had been playing with the Indian children and going in and out of their homes with them for three years.) Father felt that with me to interpret and to vouch for them, something might be done, and he was correct.

So of course when they appealed to me for assistance I, boy-like, was most receptive, for to me it offered a little change and possibly some excitement! It was known when the steamboat Michigan would be due in Little Traverse, and it was expected the paymaster would be on it, so we agreed that we would start early that morning.

Father had bought me a pony the spring before—a splendid little saddle horse—and by this time I could ride almost any horse. I was used to long rides nearly every day, so that I could ride all day without much fatigue. So that morning I started about four o'clock and rode the mile to Middle Village, where some of the Indians were waiting for me, and together we rode on to Little Traverse, arriving there about nine o'clock.

After caring for our ponies, we went to the place where the paymaster had begun paying. On seeing Mr. Blackbird, the interpreter, with whom I was acquainted, I drew him down so that I could whisper in his ear. I told him that some of the Indians whom I happened to know, and whose circumstances I knew, wanted me to speak for them, and I asked him if he would consent for me to do so.

He turned to Mr. Fitch, the paymaster, and told him that for some reason some of the Indians wanted me to interpret for them. After talking with me for a moment, Mr. Fitch consented to my doing so and directed that all those from Middle Village who wanted me to interpret for them should be attended to at once.

When we were through with them, I went away to play with some of my former Indian boy acquaintances. I had not been gone very long when Mr. Fitch sent for me to ask me what I knew about the Cross Village Indians. I told him that I had lived there a year and that I knew most of them very well. After we were through with the Cross Village contingent, Mr. Fitch said he would consider the matter and see if he could arrive at any plan by which he could get the money to those who could not appear in person to draw their pay.

Soon after arriving there than morning, I had met Mr. Richard Cooper, with whom I was acquainted, who kindly invited me to his house for dinner. At noon Mr. Fitch also came there for dinner, and as we were leaving the table he asked me to remain nearby as he wanted to see me a little later.

He and Mr. Cooper conferred together, and he wanted Mr. Cooper to take the money for the absent Indians and to see that it was paid to them later, which Mr. Cooper declined to do. After conferring together, they decided to see if I would agree to do it. I remember feeling rather squeamish about doing it, but they both encouraged me to undertake it, and promised to help me in any way I might suggest.

So finally I said that if they would engage a certain man with whom I was well acquainted, whom I felt sure I could rely on to help me, I would undertake it. The man I asked them to engage, to go with me and remain with me until I should pay over all of the money to the right persons, was Joseph Payant, who formerly had been in the employ of the Hudson Bay Fur Company for several years. I had known him intimately for about four years.

You may wonder how I can say that I was intimately acquainted with grown people, I being only a small boy. In this case, Mr. and Mrs. Payant were French, and at home always spoke French, but Peter

Paul Payant, their young son, like myself, had been very much among the Indians and could speak the Indian language very well. So could I, so when we were together we used the Indian language.

Peter had visited me at my Middle Village home a few times, for a few days each time, and I had visited him at his home even more times, and generally stayed several days, sometimes a week or more. His parents liked to have me with them, as Peter was learning some English, and I got a smattering of French. So naturally, we were well acquainted.

Mr. Payant and I agreed that we would start about 7:30 that evening. So that afternoon I rode my pony to Payants' home, which was near the foot of the bluff at the back of the village, and left the pony with him. He was to take both ponies up the hill and a little way out in the standing timber and wait for me there,

and I was to walk out there a little later. By 7:30 that evening we were on our ponies and on the trail.

The gold was sewed safely in a shot bag, and then fastened securely inside my shirt, this having been done by Mr. and Mrs. Cooper. Mr. Payant told me during our ride that he thought this mission a most unreasonable thing to ask of a little boy. He said that he had hesitated for some time before consenting to have any part in it, and had only agreed at all because he was afraid I would undertake it alone if he should refuse.

The trail was good, but so narrow at first that two could not ride abreast through the timber, but more than half the way it went through open country, old abandoned Indian gardens of a hundred years before.

About two miles before we reached Middle Village, we met an Indian and stopped for a moment. He asked me if I thought the Indians who could not go after their pay would be likely to get it. I told him I was pretty sure they would, and that they might get it the next day, but I didn't tell him that I was right then carrying it to them!

We passed through Middle Village and on to my home, where we ended our sixteen-mile ride about midnight. The next morning Mr. Payant and I went to Middle Village and took the money to those there, and after an early dinner at our house, we went to Cross Village, where I delivered the last of the nineteen twenty-dollar gold pieces for which I had felt so keenly responsible.

And for all this, it never occurred to me, and I doubt if it did to anyone else, that I was fairly entitled to a dollar, or a half dollar, or at least a nickel's worth of candy!

Reader, all this was not much, but to say the least it was unusual. So rare, in fact, that in my more than seventy three years experience, I have known of no other case where a little boy, less than eight years of age, has had the responsibility for nearly four hundred dollars thrust upon him, the money to be delivered to nineteen individuals, scattered over two villages, six miles apart, the nearest one fifteen miles from the starting point.

And all this in a wild new region, at the very moment when lawlessness and drunkenness were without restraint, and with the incentive to crime which a barrel of gold dollars poured into the streets of a little village would be. Reader, have you known of another case such as this?

Chapter 14
Changes in the Fishing Industry

The weather during the fall of 1856 was unusually fine and warm. It had been real Indian summer weather for some weeks, down to the evening before the November election. But at daylight on election morning it was snowing, although the ground was not yet white. But I think the greatest amount of snow fell in the next twenty four hours that I have ever known in more than seventy years.

The men at our place started for Cross Village to vote as soon as it was light enough to see. When they got back that evening about nine o'clock there was fully two feet of snow. One of the men became exhausted so that the others had to assist him by walking on either side and bearing most of his weight for the last mile or so. I rather think this was the first presidential election ever held in what is now Emmet County.

When this storm came, the weather turned very cold, with heavy winds, and there were three or four gangs of nets in the lake. There followed about two weeks of as hard, cold, disagreeable work as any crew of fishermen ever experienced. The shop with its open fireplace had to be utilized to thaw out the nets and fish. By the time they would reach shore, each gang of nets would be frozen into a big wad, and the fish frozen into a solid mass. Well, perhaps some of the present day fishermen have had similar experiences. If so, they can visualize the mess we were in better than I can write it.

The year 1857 saw the fishing industry assume proportions easily twice what it had ever been before. There were more men, boats and equipment engaged in it, as all now felt free to operate on as large a scale as they could handle, without fear of being stolen out or burned out of their property.

That year some man conceived the idea of a short round turned float and lead sinker, both permanently attached to the net. The advantage of this float or "cork" as it was called, and the lead sinker, appealed to every fisherman, and in one year completely displaced the old style long float and stone sinker.

At first these corks were made of cottonwood bark, but as this wood did not grow here it was expensive at best and in limited amount. So experiments were made with many other devices, and among these was a tin float. These were made of two concave tin disks, about the size and depth of an ordinary tea saucer, the edges of two disks being turned toward each other, and then soldered together so as to be air tight. These worked very well in shallow water, down to about sixteen fathoms, but were worthless in deep water, as they would collapse under heavy pressure, so they never came into general use.

Then the cedar float was tried and found to be so satisfactory that it has been about the only thing used from that time to the present, although some aluminum floats have been used in recent years.

In the year 1858, someone invented the pound net, which in my opinion proved to be a great curse to the fishing industry. Probably not more than four or five of these nets were used in this part of Lake Michigan that year, but the next year a great many—probably more than a hundred—were set in this part of the lake.

The far sighted fishermen got their orders in early for a net, and then quietly bought and bargained for barrels, wherever they were to be had. Owing to the extraordinary demand for barrels that fall, the price went from fifty cents up to ninety cents. Some had five hundred barrels, or even a thousand, on hand when fall came, but some found when the time came to use them that there were none to be had.

To give you some idea of the use of the pound net for shoal fishing, I am going to tell you a "fish story". You may find it hard to believe that it could have been the experience of even one man, but it really was. This man, by the name of William Crane, got his net in good time and decided to set it near us at the Middle Village fishing grounds. But by the time he had his net set, he was unable to find any barrels.

Now imagine, if you can, what would—or did—happen. Imagine a mass of fish entering through that funnel, wiggling, pushing, crowding in, until it was literally a solid mass. Then, from sheer pressure, it burst a large hole in the side of the pot, through which the fish escaped. Men who were out to the net the day before it burst said that the top of the mass of fish was fully a foot above the surface of the lake, and these fish were dead.

The destruction of fish lay not so much in the myriads of fish taken as in the barrels upon barrels of spawn that were carried away with the offal and buried. In a given time a single pound net would gather in more fish that were ready to spawn than a hundred gill nets could have done. I am quite sure that many of the fisheries could have saved a barrel of ripe spawn a day for several days in succession, but it was not done. With such wicked waste going on, year after year, what wonder is it that in ten years pound nets would not catch enough fish to pay operating expenses?

Isn't it strange that man, who is supposed to be endowed with reasoning faculties, should wreck such destruction and loss upon himself and his environment? Think of the utter annihilation of the wild pigeons, the near extinction of the buffalo, the beaver, the whitefish, trout and sturgeon, as well as the wonderful forests and the many other useful gifts of nature. But with these examples staring humanity in the face, the destruction and devastation still goes on, almost with unabated fury!

I began this chapter by telling you of the stormy weather we had during the winter of 1856-57. It is true our weather was, and is, sometimes cold and stormy, but in the experience of many people it has also proved to be healthful and invigorating.

My mother had come west to Detroit from Rochester, New York, with her older brother, Steven Hull. A year later her other two brothers, Horace and Daniel, came. Later, those two brothers went to Toledo and still later to New Orleans where, after two or three years' residence, they were both stricken with yellow fever and Daniel died.

Horace recovered from the fever but was left broken in health, and soon developed a bad lingering cough. After becoming convinced that he could not live long there, he returned north to Toledo in hopes that he would benefit by the change of climate.

For a year or two Mother had written, urging him several times to come up here to us. So the spring of 1858 he came on the first boat, barely able to walk

74

a few rods. The first few days he was with us he could hardly walk across the room. But soon he began to eat with relish and by the time he had been with us three months, there was no cough and he was gaining flesh and strength rapidly. That fall he filled an able man's place at fishing.

I have seen others come into this region in the same or worse condition, people who could hardly walk or speak without difficulty in breathing, who could scarcely eat or sleep , with the "shadow of the valley" their only hope of relief. And then I have seen them months afterwards, when their former extreme condition was but a memory, and some of them thirty or forty years afterward, full of robust health.

Chapter 15
My Friends the Surveyors

During the late spring of 1857, a government surveying party established their camp within a few rods of where we were living. They had begun this survey during the late summer and fall of 1856, immediately following the treaty with the Indians of Little Traverse.

It seems probable that the land south of what is now township Number 31 north in the different ranges west, from Lake Michigan easterly for a distance of several townships, had been surveyed as early as 1841. It appears by records kindly furnished to me by Mr. R. F. Sloan of Charlevoix, that townships Number 33 of Range 4 west and Number 34 of range 6 west (and probably Numbers 31, 32 and 33) were surveyed in 1841 also. I think that this crooked zigzag line would mark the southern boundary line of this tract which had recently been Indian reserve land.

However, surveying had been done in a few places at a much earlier date, possibly in the 1830's or earlier, at Little Traverse and Cross Village, where villages had been platted, and I think, at Cheboygan and Duncan City, where villages had been platted and sawmills built.

There must have been as many as fifteen men, including carpenters, in the land survey crew which settled near us, and I think they were there for as much as six weeks. A lake survey of this part of the lake was also being made at the same time.

The government lake survey boat was a beautiful, medium size, sidewheel steamboat. After their work for the day was done, and if the weather was nice, the men would come to anchor in the offing and come ashore. There the two crews visited and frolicked—sometimes all night!

The cook of the land crew used to stay at the camp during the day, and he and I got to be pretty good pals. You might be interested in learning something about our bill of fare in the early days. Knowing that little was produced but fish hereabouts, it might seem that our fare might narrow down to just bread, potatoes and fish, but such was not the case.

Immediately after moving into the lighthouse that first spring, my parents bought something like a dozen hens from the Indians, and we were never without hens after that. Each spring a little pig was raised up to be a fine young porker by fall. For most of the year the hens kept us in eggs and all the chicken we could care for. The pig furnished spareribs and sausage for the holiday season and fresh pork all winter.

Rabbits, partridges and wild ducks were very plentiful and wild pigeons by the millions. Sometimes, though not often, we would get a wild goose. There were lots of squirrels—black, gray, fox and red—and other small game. There were no game laws then, so hunting was different than it is today. Then, if one went out for a couple of hours, he might bring back as much small game as he could carry. On the mainland, there were plenty of deer and some bear.

There was an abundance of wild fruit, such as

apples, plums, cherries (red and black), blackberries, strawberries, raspberries, grapes, currants, huckleberries, gooseberries, and cranberries—all in unlimited supply. Some were dried and some made into fine preserves and jams for winter.

In 1857 the knack of canning fruits was developed. When they came up in the spring of 1858, our missionary friends, the Turners, brought us a dozen one-gallon tin cans, which we were very glad to get. The cans had a screw cap in the center of the top, with the rubber ring much like those in use now. But those large, awkward tin cans soon gave way to the half-gallon, quart, and pint glass jars in use today.

Maple sugar and syrup were in such quantity and so cheap that tons of it was shipped to Chicago and the eastern cities. At Mackinac we could buy anything that could be found in any city from Chicago to Buffalo.

So you can see that with bread and pastries, potatoes, beans, squash, beets, cabbage, green corn, corned beef, smoked ham and bacon, salt pork, and all kinds of freshwater fish, we could and did have everything at its best that anybody anywhere could have. Whatever difference there was in the table fare was owing to the difference there was in the women behind the scheme of things in the different homes, and my mother was a good cook and housekeeper!

Both survey crews seemed to like me and made much of me. One day my parents consented to my going with the lake crew on the steamboat, and one other day I was with the land crew when they were surveying not far away.

The carpenters built a very high observation tower on the brink of that great cliff, not more than a quarter of a mile from us, and I spent much of my time with them. I heard them say that the observation platform of this tower was the highest above the water level that they had built anywhere.

In each of these crews of men were some who gave me books and magazines and papers. There were not many daily papers published in the United States in those days. Owing to lack of mail facilities, they would not have been of much use to us. But weekly publications were taken by nearly all fishermen. Each trader that left Mackinac would take the mail for all whom he would be likely to see on that cruise, so our mail would reach us once a month or oftener during the season of navigation.

Some of the books these men gave me were sufficiently advanced to meet the requirements of postgraduate students, but for all that, I think they did me some good. I continued to get books from some of them for four or five years. When these surveyors left our place, I experienced the first sense of loss that I ever felt.

I think that Captain George G. Mead, who had charge of this land survey outfit, was the General George G. Mead who served under General U. S. Grant in the Civil War, but give it only as my opinion.

Chapter 16
Missionaries in the Family

As this narrative has developed, I have told you something about the Indians and quite a bit about the fishermen who made up most of the population in these early days. But I would be remiss in my obligation to you if I did not at least touch upon the great contribution made by the missionaries toward the development of the region.

Late in the fall of 1857, our friends and only white neighbors, Mr. and Mrs. Turner, the missionaries, went back to Cincinnati to spend the winter, so we were alone at Middle Village for another winter. The nearest white families were at Little Traverse, sixteen miles distant, and as we were keeping a cow and chickens, it was impossible for us to go there to visit them. But these friends got ponies and drove to our place several times to visit us that winter, generally staying with us three or four days each time.

In the meantime, there were more settlers at Pine River. In October of 1857, S.F. Mason and family and M.J. Stockman and his wife took up land on the south side of Round Lake, the combined area reaching from what is now State Street to Pine Lake. (Mr. Mason lost his life November 15, 1870, trying to enter the river on a very stormy night. Missing the river, he collided with Fox's and Rose's dock, and in some way he was killed in the wreck.)

The first boat up in the spring of 1858 brought Mr. and Mrs. Turner and their first baby, little Emma. With them was also a young lady, Miss Theodocia Mc-Grue, a niece of Mr. Turner. The same boat brought my mother's brother, Mr. Horace Hull, whom I have mentioned before, who became acquainted with the Turners and their niece. The acquaintance between him and Miss McGrue ripened into friendship and then into love, and they were married June 8th of that year.

Mr. and Mrs. Turner never quite became reconciled to the humdrum missionary life, and now that they had a child to consider, they decided that summer to give it up and return to Cincinnati to stay. Their niece's marriage made it possible for them to depart earlier than they had expected to do, as they could leave the mission in charge of Mr. and Mrs. Hull.

Mr. Hull's appointment as missionary dated from the time the Turners left and gave the young couple an income of four hundred dollars a year. Mrs. Hull was a very estimable lady, beloved by all who came to know her, for her modest womanly graces and her kindness.

The young married couple bought the entire housekeeping equipment from the Turners, and thus was established without the usual trials of house hunting, buying furniture, and getting settled. Neither was there the discouragement of hunting for a job.

It was required of the missionaries that they provide one church service each Sunday, that they keep school half a day each day for three months of the year, and that they visit the sick and needy occasionally. You might imagine that such a life might be rather prosaic. But when Mr. Hull took over the care of the mission property, he made the hay that was growing on the place, saved such other feed as he could, and bought a cow and a nice flock of hens. Thus they were assured of a supply of milk, cream, butter, eggs and chickens. That fall they brought a few things and lived in a little house near us, and he worked for Father at fishing.

This same year, 1858, Mr. Andrew Porter, the missionary at Bear Creek, built a water power grist mill on that creek (where Petoskey is now located). This helped him to pass the time and made life there somewhat less monotonous. Now, you may reasonably wonder where the grist would come from, and you may be surprised when I tell you that the grain came from southwest Michigan, northern Indiana and Missouri, Illinois and Wisconsin.

In the years that this story covers, there were thousands of vessels engaged in carrying lumber from the Michigan mills to Chicago and Milwaukee, and in carrying grain from these cities to Buffalo and other eastern cities. Every year, this tremendous lake commerce resulted in many wrecks. It was no unusual thing for from fifteen to thirty thousand bushels of dry wheat, corn and oats to be salvaged in a single fall, and generally much more of wet grain which, when dried, made good feed for livestock, and this grain made many grists for the Little Bear Creek mill.

I have known as many as a thousand barrels of flour to be salvaged from a single wreck. Every year hundreds of barrels of flour were saved in this way.

In just a few years, the lumber that came ashore on the east shore of Lake Michigan furnished material for many of the buildings and Mackinaw boats that people needed. As you may recall Father's first set of buildings at Middle Village, as well as the school house and missionary's dwelling there, had been constructed from some of this salvaged lumber, purchased from the Indians.

I have one more little note about the Hulls. On June 10, 1859, they became parents of a son, John, who after weathering the vicissitudes incident to pioneer childhood and youth, finally grew to manhood and became one of our fellow townsmen in Charlevoix.

Not only did the missionaries give generously of their time and abilities to the general well being of the area, but several of them also contributed to my personal well being and education. Mr. Turner gave me such books as the mission afforded, including a dictionary. He was a subscriber to an educational magazine of that time, and he had one year's issues bound, which he also gave to me.

Mr. Porter of the Bear Creek mission sent me a large atlas, and a fine History of the United States, which covered Columbus and his discoveries, the first settlements, the colonies, and on down to the year 1860.

Rev. H.W. Guthries, the Presbyterian minister who alternated between the Bear Creek and Middle Village missions one year, gave me quite a comprehensive work on astronomy and one on botany.

In 1863, when we were living six miles south of Elk Rapids in a little hamlet known as Yuba, there was a Congregational minister, Rev. Leroy Warren, who gave me many good books; and one lovable old minister, Rev. Thompson from Benzonia, who had been for many years a missionary in Africa, gave me three very interesting books on Africa, one large volume of which he was the author.

And before I was seven years old, I became in-

terested in the Bible, an interest which has never died
out. I think I studied it with as much devotion, hon-
esty of purpose, and desire to learn the truth as anyone
could. Never having been under the influence of any
church or Sunday School, nor of religionists of any cult
or sect or "ism", I think I was as free as anyone could
be from bias, bigotry, superstition, fear, dogmatism,
or prejudice—either for or against—or from any of the
other follies that have been inbred in the human mind
since eons before Genesis was written.

The time came when I believed I understood every essential, vital truth the Bible teaches. I still think
so. It teaches salvation in a most reasonable way, and I
trust it implicitly. Whatever confusion and misunder-
standing has arisen in the world has been of the student's own making, and not because the Bible's teaching itself is confusing.

Chapter 17
The Schoolroom Doors Bang Shut

As we are nearing the end of this narration, I think I ought to remind you that with the end of 1859, I am almost eleven years old, and nowhere have I been able to record my attendance at any school. The only one that I have seen so much as the outside of is the little mission school standing back of Middle Village at the edge of the forest. I will give you a sort of running account of the few crumbs of schooling that I have picked up along the way, although I shall have to reach over into the next decade to do so.

At the close of the fishing season in the fall of 1859, Father had the men go with the boat, taking our household effects and the nets to Little Traverse, leaving everything else behind. He hired an Indian to lead our cow, and we drove with my pony and sleigh, and settled at Little Traverse.

The Government had built a schoolhouse, and was maintaining school there, and my parents thought that I would get fair schooling. But a couple of days or so before we came, the teacher, having decided to quit, boarded the last boat south. So there was not school that winter, and I drew a blank.

A year later the Government sent a teacher named Dennis T. Downing. It was very late in the fall when he came, and he decided not to have a winter term, so that was that! The next spring he opened school, and I was there. But at the close of school that Saturday noon (the school week was then five and a half days) he sent word by me to Father, requesting that he see him before the next Monday, which he did.

Mr. Downing informed Father that he was hired to teach only Indians, and that he couldn't keep me as a pupil. Father was willing to pay any reasonable tuition fee, but there was nothing doing! So I was a little more than twelve years old before I ever held a book in my hand inside a school, and that for only one week! But I was very grateful for that week.

It was some time after this that I found out what had made him decide against me, and then only because his son, Tommy, and I were real pals. He was a good kid, just two or three months older than I, and a real sport. One day when we were together, I asked him if he knew why his father wouldn't admit me to the school. After a moment's hesitation, he said, "Yes, I do, and Mother and I don't like it either. It's because you are a much better scholar than I am. You never have had any schooling, and yet you are way ahead of me, and I think it has got me several lickings!" Tommy was the first white boy playmate I had ever had, and I was almost twelve years old when he came here.

At the close of the spring term of 1862, Mr. Downing gave up the school at Little Traverse, and Mr. William Homer Fife of Yuba, Grand Traverse County, was appointed teacher. He arrived there during the summer, and in September began a fall term of school.

Well, here's the way that worked out. The Homestead Law had been passed, and Father had been exposed to it, had been thoroughly inoculated, and at this time was at the very height of the fever! But he was undecided where to locate the land. Mr. Fife recommended his part of the country, and thought that good land could be obtained within reach of some school already established. So we moved again, after I had had about ten days in Mr. Fife's school, and landed at Yuba the first day of October, 1862.

That winter I got less than two weeks school, and the following summer (1863) I had about two weeks more. The spring of 1864, we moved to Deep Water Point, nearly a mile north of Acme, and there again I had two weeks in school. The last day of September we left there, bound for Pine River, where Father had finally decided to enter his Homestead claim, and had done so the April before. We landed at Pine River the morning of October first, 1864, exactly two years from the day we had landed at Yuba.

When we had been on the homestead a couple of years, a teacher was hired and a little abandoned shack was pressed into service, and once more I attended school. But the third or fourth day the teacher told me confidentially that I would be wasting my time in that school unless I would consent to be her teacher!

Although she thought she might be able to help me a little in grammar, she felt it would consume too much time to send outside for a textbook. So I left school at the end of the first week, which left six students, among them a boy my own age to the day, for whose needs the teacher felt herself perfectly qualified.

This good little woman cried when I had to leave the school because of her own deficient education. This was a few years after the development of this region was in full swing, and when there were schools in most of the townships of this north country.

Well, it was beginning to look rather discouraging to me, for I wanted very much to have at least a common school education, and it seemed that I would have to earn the money with which to go somewhere else to get it, but this I was never able to do.

However, during the winter of 1869 and 1870, Major E.H. Green taught a twelve-weeks term of school in what had by then been named Charlevoix. The little schoolhouse stood exactly where State and Antrim Streets now cross, and was half on the original plat of Charlevoix and half off.

A most primitive school it was, but Major Green was a most capable and excellent teacher—indeed, a splendid man in all that makes for splendid manhood. I cherish his memory more than I can tell.

I had the benefit of eleven weeks at this school, which did me a world of good, but I was obliged to lose the last week to start the maple sugar making. At this point I was twenty one years old, and this ended my formal education once and for all.

But I did have my books. As I have indicated before, traders, acquaintances, surveyors and missionaries gave me books. A very complete work on natural philosophy came to me from the first captain of the splendid new wrecking tug, Leviathan, a man whose name I have forgotten. I think this book has helped me more in my lifetime than any other single book.

For many years, books continued to come to me, books on many subjects. By this time I had also begun buying books for myself, mostly books on the different sciences. Friend Reader, it may seem to you that I am describing a perfect deluge of books. Well, I don't know how many there were, but there were a lot of them—maybe a couple of hundred. And I can truly say that there was not one book that should have been censored out of any company or family.

I did not give these books merely a superficial reading. Nearly all were studied as a devoted student would study them, with the hope of learning some useful truth. And some of those sciences—shall I say it?—I mastered!

Yes, Friend, I have stood before some fine audiences and held their interested attention for an hour or more, lecturing on some of those sciences—often the subject of their own choosing; and I have always believed that the compliments following these lectures were sincere.

Chapter 18
Why We Came

Last evening, just seventy years almost to the exact day since that April of 1852 when this story begins, I laid this writing aside to spend the evening with two old friends of long ago, and this is the story.

On the trip on the steamer Michigan that spring of 1852 was a little girl of eight years of age who had been sent to friends in Cleveland, Ohio, the fall before for a winter's schooling. Coming up on the boat, she and I and my parents became friends, and we have been friends ever since.

She was coming back to this "awful country" as many people called it in those days. Last evening, in talking over old times, her voice trembled when she was telling that one of the greatest joys of her life was when we reached Mackinac, the place of her birth, and again when we reached Beaver Island, her home at that time.

Reader, if to live here in the wilds at that time would be such a terrible experience, why should she not have preferred Cleveland with its modern society, its wealth, its schools and churches—but also its vice, noise, confusion and dirt? Have you any idea what the lure was, and is?

What is it that has coaxed so many young men and women away from comfort and civilization, sometimes from home and friends, out to the Great Plains, into the mountains, the frozen north or the torrid south, to endure privation and hardship and loneliness? Just what was the pull?

Neighbor, I have been through it all—everything that this great region had to offer—and it was not lacking in anything pertaining to a frontier. So if you ask me what is so enticing about a new country, I shall have to say that in an old country or large city you can see little or nothing of God's handiwork. The city may be very beautiful as a work of art, but it has lost the magnetism of nature. But in the new country, in the great spaces of God's unspoiled wilderness, with you as the sole representative of all humanity, you see and are part of all that He has made.

The close of the decade of the 1850's found us living at Little Traverse, making our final footprints in the sand. I think this story should end at that point, because the year 1860 marked the beginning of the development which has given to you and me this beautiful modernized region as we have it today and should be the subject of another story.

The sixty two years which have passed since that time are rich in adventure, in humorous and pathetic episodes, in real bravery and hardihood, in hope and despair, in success and failure, in labor and love and fruition.

We awake in the early morning of a new era, a new dispensation in fact, for this region, and we reverently bow and give thanks to a kind Providence, and ask His blessing on our new line of endeavor.

We took our place with the other new arrivals, took possession, and began the development of a new country. In the years that have passed, I have seen it developed and exploited and modernized until, as we have it today, it has lost all semblance of its former self.

And now, young people, at the beginning of this happy and prosperous New Year of Nineteen Hundred and Twenty Three, we dedicate to you the results of these long years of labor and love, privation and fruition, for you to enjoy and improve and pass along to those who will come after you.

The End

Afterword

My Grandfather was completing his manuscript during the autumn and early winter of 1922 just as I was entering into this world! Could he have known that it would take 88 years before his stories were finally published?

During my early years, Grandpa Stevie as we called him was busy with his neighborhood grocery store. Along with Grandma Hattie, they were storekeepers for 10 years. After my grandmother's sudden death in 1929, (Grandfather was then 80 years old) my parents (Arthur & Mildred Staley) moved into the living quarters behind the store and became storekeepers. Grandfather spent his final years with my parents, sisters and me living here. Twenty years later, my wife Arlene & I became storekeepers until we closed the store in 1983.

The store building had been constructed from materials moved via boat from Cross Village by the Crandall's. When the store was first built at 401 Antrim Street, it was on the highway! At that time, traffic crossed the bridge, followed Bridge Street to Antrim Street, and turned right to Sheridan Street, then left, crossing what is now the airport, on to Barnard and Norwood to what is now the Old Dixie Highway. The little store was one of five neighborhood grocery stores in Charlevoix during the mid 1900's. The original living quarters were on the second story before a lean-to addition was added on three sides. Later remodeling that took place discovered wavy window glass, heavy hand carved counters, etc.

Prior to purchasing the store in 1919 from the Crandall's, Grandfather acquired properties around the City of Charlevoix. Like his father before him, he was well respected and served as justice of the peace and in other civic offices. He told of building his parents home during an especially warm winter in the 1880's. This homestead was built on land acquired in 1864 from the Federal Government. It is near the site of the new high school on Marion Center Road.

There was an old "McCasky" file in the store that was used to keep the records of the accounts receivable. I asked Grandfather about the considerable number of accounts which were unpaid. He said that most of the people who owed him money were in such dire circumstance, compared to him, that the accounts need not be of concern any longer. He said, "I am in better shape than any of those people." He did not expect to be paid and the spirit of giving to those less fortunate was one to which he had been introduced at a very young age.

93

When Grandfather was in his late eighties, he would often sit near the rear of the store and observe as customers came and went. I recall how he would become excited and talkative when an elderly Indian lady, Mrs. Oliver, would enter the store. He would greet her in her language "BooZuu!" from the back of the store! They would communicate in the Indian language and enjoy each other's company and their common bonds. It was more like a class reunion as they were interested in what was happening in each other's lives since the last meeting! Mrs. Oliver had worked for a furrier in Traverse City during her earlier days. Her son, Jay, became an elder at the Greensky Hill Indian Mission Church near Charlevoix. Jay's recorded recitation of the Lord's Prayer can still be heard in the Indian language every Sunday morning during the 9 o'clock service at Greensky Hill Church. The Indian language was not written until 1887 when Andrew Jackson Blackbird, Odawa tribal leader and historian, wrote the first dictionary and history of the tribes. The Doxology, printed in the Indian language, hangs in the church and its fellowship hall. It is sung each week after the offering is taken.

Recently, my wife & I took a ride to the lake shore area called Middle Village which is about a mile south of Good Hart and on the shore of Lake Michigan. I had taken my sisters there more than 25 years ago when my sister Audrey was doing research for this book. There is a footpath access from the small Church to the lakeshore now. We saw the cove where, in the fall of 1855, a house and cooper shop were built for the young Smith family. This very well could have been Stephen's introduction to "Indian 101" as he had no brothers or sisters yet. With his mother being an English teacher and his playmates being Indian, this environment provided the perfect setting for language studies for young Stephen! This early introduction to the Indian language was beneficial when he was witness to the treaty making between the Federal Government agents and the Indian Chiefs in 1856. His early interest in learning was aided by regular deliveries of books and materials from Government vessels, missionaries, surveyors and traders who frequented the Smith household. His early education included subjects such as astronomy, psychology and philosophy. His studies were often far above his expected abilities.

I am happy to see my Grandfather's stories in print. It has been a long time wish of the family to share the stories of his experiences growing up as a pioneer in Michigan's northwest region.

Kenneth A. Staley, 2011

Appendix A

Strange "King" Strang and Mrs. Bloomer's Bloomers
An Episode AWAY OFF "the Road to Zion"

By Stephen Smith, Sole Survivor of the "Kingdom"

This is a reprint of a story that was printed in The American Weekly on September 1, 1940. The story, with pictures, spanned nearly three newspaper sized pages! One Headline read: "The True Story of a Little-Known "Mormon Monarchy" On an Island in Lake Michigan, and How It Flourished Despite All Sorts of Oppressions and Cruelties, Till Its Pretentious Little Ruler Made the Fatal Error of Trying to Force All the Women in His Realm to Wear Pants". Some drawings from the article are included. s/ Editor.

Readers of the American Weekly who followed Mr. Joseph E. Robinson's epic account of the Mormon migration, "The Road to Zion," concluded two weeks ago in this magazine, will recall that after the assassination of Joseph Smith several Mormon elders attempted to set themselves up as the Prophet's successor, and that when Brigham Young was chosen, some of the others became disgruntled and refused to follow the new leader.

One of those who broke away was James Jesse Strang, a man of small stature but big ideas, who gathered together a following and not only borrowed the Mormon name for his new religious sect, but also took over Beaver Island in Lake Michigan and established an "absolute monarchy," with himself as "king".

So far as can be determined, there is living today only one survivor of strange "King" Strang's ambitious "kingdom". He is 91-year-old Stephen Smith, whose people were not members of Strang's church, but whose father lived on the island as keeper of the "royal" lighthouse.

From his home in Charlevoix, Michigan, Mr. Smith has written his vivid and dramatic account of this somewhat quaint but tragic experiment in totalitarian government in our democratic country; and it is presented here as an interesting and unique footnote to a little-known chapter in American history, quite a way off of "The Road to Zion".

Ninety-One years old, I am! And so far as I know, I'm the only one now alive who ever saw the "King" of Beaver Island.

Yes, sir, a kingdom right in the United States of America!

I lived in that kingdom in Lake Michigan for several years as a young shaver and saw terrible things; things you'd never believe possible in this free country. My father and mother went there to take over the lighthouse after King James Jesses Strang drove out the old lighthouse keeper, and when we landed at St. James (The king said he was a saint too!), the first man I saw was the king himself, sitting on a salt barrel.

He was short, about five feet four, but mighty hefty looking. He had bright red hair and a great carroty beard. His face, with high, bulging forehead, was white like red headed peoples' skins are sometimes, and his eyes, under bushy brows, were small, pale and cold as ice. They seemed to look right through me. I went to him, I didn't want to, but something seemed to make me. He picked me up and put me on his knee.

"D'you know who I am?" he asked.

"You're the king," I answered.

He seemed to swell and his great, big knuckled hands gripped me until they hurt.

"I'm afraid of you!" And I began to cry.

He let me down and I ran to my mother. (I was only three and a half years old.)

After that, he often came to the lighthouse to talk to my father and mother, but they were afraid of him too and so was everyone else on that island.

He killed any number of men and women, and had others tied up and flogged 'til they bled. He sent men to loot gentile stores and even had pirates sailing around the island to rob the fishing boats. He let on that he was a prophet of God, but he was more like one of those dictators you hear so much about nowadays. He said he was the Law on Beaver Island, and all the people who lived there had to do like he said, even when it was against the law of the United States.

But he was killed in the end, and after all the bloodshed he caused and all the power he had, the reason they shot him was over an article he read in an Eastern newspaper. He'd read of that woman, Mrs. Amelia Bloomer she was, who started wearing pantaloons because, she said, they were more healthy than dresses.

Well, nothing would do but all the women on his island had to wear bloomers, as they were called. And then—

But I'm getting ahead of myself; I'll begin at the beginning.

James Jesse Strang was born in Scipio, Cayuga County, New York, on March 21, 1813. His family moved to Hanover in Chautauqua County and there he went to school. He was always a small kid, and like most little people he was mighty uppity and ambitious. Whenever he could get time off from his farm work he read law books, and then later went to Fredonia Academy to study for a lawyer. It wasn't long before he hung out his shingle in Ellington County. They made him postmaster after a bit and when he'd made enough money, he married Mary Pierce.

That was the beginning of the happenings that led him through all his trouble.

His wife's brother had done well for himself in Burlington, Wisconsin, and Strang, not to be outdone by him, took his bride to the same place. He met a lawyer, C.C. Barnes, and started in partners with him. But the law business in that small town was not enough to satisfy young Strang.

He was always kind of restless and looking out for some big chance that would make him important. One day he heard about the Mormon Church, which was already attracting a lot of attention. Joseph Smith was the head of it. The idea of a new religion excited Strang and in January, 1844, he hit the trail for Nauvoo, the Mormon headquarters in Southern Illinois. He decided to join and Joseph Smith himself baptized the little man through a hole cut in the ice of the swampland outside Nauvoo.

Strang wasted no time. He went to every meeting of the elders and it wasn't long before he made his presence felt. Only a week later Smith made him too an elder in the church which gave him the right to plant a "Stake in Zion". That meant he could go anywhere he liked and start a place of his own where he could collect converts and be in charge of them. That gave him his chance. He would be like bigger men. He'd be bigger than any of them.

He chose Burlington for his "Zion" because he already had a small following there and he named it Voree, the "Garden of Peace".

But it wasn't a Garden of Peace for long!

(Joseph) Smith was killed soon after and there were several elders who had started "Stakes in Zion" in different places. Strang, always looking for a chance to make himself more powerful, showed a letter that he said Smith had written a week before he died and which left him the leadership of the Mormons. But five other elders said they had letters too.

Well, the Mormons at Nauvoo had a lot of arguments among the elders but finished up by choosing Brigham Young as their leader. And eventually he (Young) ordered them to follow him on a great trek to Utah.

This made Strang mad as hops. He raved and preached at the people, promising them everlasting peace and prosperity if they'd only go with him. Some did and soon Burlington had a good size company of Mormons in it. He chose a council of "apostles" and a dozen elders and sent them out as missionaries.

They roamed the East and mid-West and brought many converts to Voree. Strang talked to every one of them, checking up and measuring to find how much good they'd be to him.

For he had a plan, a plan as high flown as any dictator ever thought of. He would be a king, and Burlington was to be his kingdom. He even made plans for a tabernacle and his apostles went out to find people to build it for him.

Wisconsin at this time had just been admitted to the Union, and the gentiles, which they called all those who didn't belong to the Mormon Church, began to feel scared of the strangers who were taking over their land. But Strang wouldn't let anything interfere with his plans.

No sir! Napoleon was a little man, he remembered, and he'd become an emperor. Well, James Jesse Strang would be another, and no thing on earth would stop him. He figured that sooner or later the gentiles would break up his disciples and drive them out of Wisconsin. So he started looking about for a place where they'd be safe. He remembered a beautiful island in Lake Michigan which he'd seen from a ship some years before. There weren't many folk on it so it looked like a cinch for his "Garden of Peace".

In May 1847 he started out in a small boat with four apostles and on the 11th day they landed on Beaver Island. It was 13 miles long by six wide, wild and covered with maple and pine. To the nor'east was a small, landlocked bay which they used for their harbor. To the west of that were a few fishermen's shacks. There weren't many, just shacks, shanties and a store or two.

Strang took over, cool as you please and named it St. James, after himself. That will show you he was thinking more of his own future than the will of God. This little village, he said, would be the beginning of a mighty kingdom.

He left two apostles and with the other two went back to the mainland. He preached to his Mormons telling them that God had shown him a land flowing with milk and honey where there was room for all true Mormons to be happy and prosperous. By Fall, 17 men and 48 women and kids had moved to the island.

But that wasn't enough for King James. He went back for more, and returned to the island in the Spring with a big crowd. They found a number of pilgrims dead of cold and hunger. They had been set down on a strange island with no time to build decent homes before the cold Winter set in, and if it hadn't been for the gentile fishermen, they all would have starved to death. Some of them complained to King Strang but he grinned at them through his tight mouth.

"You must learn to endure hardships," he said.

And that was all he seemed to think of his people's suffering.

Well, he started in the Spring of 1849 to make Beaver Island a proper stronghold. He told his pilgrims that the land was theirs, where they would never be disturbed, where they would find everlasting peace and comfort. He ordered them to be friendly with the gentiles and share all they had with them. The Mormons got on well with the fishermen because they were good workers. They tilled the land, built roads and homes for themselves.

But the gentiles were suspicious about the pilgrims. They had heard about the outlandish practice of polygamy. They didn't want people like that living near them, and went to Strang about it. The king treated them gently. Some of his followers, he said, did have more than one wife. But they had married them before they joined him, so he couldn't very well make

102

them give up the extra women. But he said he had received revelations from God which had told him that no new converts would be allowed more than one wife. The gentiles were satisfied, but they didn't know that Strang's promises were like piecrust---made to be broken.

The king didn't spend much time on the island for the first two years. He traveled about the Eastern States appointing agents and apostles until he had a mighty crowd of converts on the island. While he was away he put George A. Adams in charge to look out for things. Adams had been a play actor in Boston before he met Strang, and he gallivanted about the island in fancy robes he used to wear on the stage.

It was in July, 1850, that James Jesse Strang, in a tabernacle he had had built in St. James, actually had himself crowned "Prophet, King and priest" of the Garden of Peace, Beaver Island. Adams, all decked out in his play-acting robes played the part of the one who did the crowning. And July 8th was set aside as "King's Day". And it's known as King's Day right up to the present time, although the people don't have a holiday or anything.

And there he was, a king.

Just as much as a European king. Then he started a reign that sounds more like one of those ancient, bloody kings of the Middle Ages, than an American man. He started a new teaching. His people stood about the tabernacle with Adams while Strang yelled and shouted to them of visitations from the Lord. (I wonder why the

Lord didn't strike him dead!)

All the teaching came from the Old Testament, he said. The Mormons were the "Peculiar People of the Lord" and all others on the island were Amelekites, who in biblical times were thieving wanderers like gypsies. It was lawful, Strang ordered, that his people should "despoil and smite" the gentiles. That was "a revelation from God". (Editor's note: despoil and smite means to plunder and hit hard.)

Imagine that! A little, red-whiskered fellow ruling hundreds of people and passing laws like that. For "Despoil and Smite" (those were his very words) was a law from then on. The fishermen couldn't do a thing about it; there weren't many of them and Strang's men were all over the place. They went into fishermen's homes without even knocking. They took what they wanted without a thank you. Then they started mobbing those who wouldn't join their group and be baptized according to the laws of King James Jesse Strang.

The king ordered that every fisherman living on the island should pay him ten dollars a year tax. And he sent out big, tough bullies with guns to see that they paid. It was just like the gangsters, a few years ago, when they sent "muscle men" to beat up the poor folk who couldn't pay protection money.

It was about that time that I first went to the island. One fisherman named Thomas Bennet refused to pay the tax. With two of his brothers, Bennet went to the lake to take in his nets. He returned about noon and was working about his house when two mighty ugly looking customers with revolvers called him and said that the king had sent them to collect his tax.

"I want to see the king before I pay taxes," said Bennet.

The two men walked away.

A few minutes later Bennet went outside and those two murderers started shooting at him from the bushes. Seven bullets hit him and he dropped dead. His brother, Sam, ran out and they shot him too, through the hand. His poor wife was hiding in the cellar, frightened out of her wits. Those two gangsters dragged Tom's body to his boat and slung it over the cargo of fish which he hadn't had time to take out.

They made Sam sit there too and took him and his wife to St. James. The body of the murdered man was thrown into a blacksmith shop to wait until they found time to bury it. A few days later they stuffed it into a deal (pine) box and buried it without a word of prayer in a grove of cedars near the shore. The boat and Bennet's catch of fish were handed over to the king.

The other fishermen were scared to death when they heard of that murder. They let Strang's men take whatever they wanted. They tried to get news to the mainland, but they couldn't get help from there, for Strang's men watched every boat that came to the island and shot every man they didn't wanted to land.

So they went on for some years. That little fellow ruled everybody with the power of his sharp little eyes. They were all in mortal fear of him; not only the gentiles but the Mormons too. For any little disobedience of his harsh laws, he ordered floggings and seldom a day went by without screams coming from the woods behind St. James.

He used to lash a pole between two trees and tie folks to it like suckling pigs. One day he flogged two men and a woman. Seventy-five lashes he gave them with what are called the "blue beeches". After the flogging they were left there, groaning and crying and no one was allowed to go near them for days. But the gentiles usually crept out in the night to help people he had used this way. The poor tortured people drank the water they brought but begged the gentiles not to say anything or they would be flogged again for taking help.

"Blue beeches" are long thin strips of beech wood peeled from trunks of beech trees. In strips, it's a pliable wood and one of the strongest kinds in our part of the country. Whips about four feet long were made out of several strips about half an inch wide, tied at the end to form a handle. These whips were not made specially to flog Strang's people but were common on Beaver Island. They were mostly used to drive horses and cattle, but old King Strang found them right handy for thrashing the members of his flock who made him mad. Although it is not always true, the wood sometimes has a bluish cast, and that's why they call them "blue beeches".

About this time King James Jesse Strang broke out with another law and this was when he first started trouble for himself. For he said that the Lord had told him that all Mormon men should take as many wives as they could. Well, the married women were fit to be tied. They went to the tabernacle and demanded to see the king. At first he wouldn't talk to them, but they just camped there 'til he came out.

"It's a revelation from God!" he bellowed at them. "I'm going to take several wives myself!"

He did too! But his lawful wife who had put up with him for years, had had enough. She packed her things and left him; went among the other women and tried to make them keep their husbands from having more women. Then she went to the mainland, for she feared Strang, and only came back to the island when he was away.

King James took four more wives. Two of them were sisters, and they seemed to be quite happy with him. He had one favorite wife though, like one of those Sultans, and she was called Charles Douglas. I don't know why he gave her a man's name. But she dressed like a man, in a black suit and high hat. She cut her hair short and went everywhere that Strang went.

One family that was all broken up over Strang's polygamy law was the Halls. Mrs. Hall got her husband to promise that he'd never bring another woman into her home. Strang got mad and tried to make her let other women come in, but there was nothing doing; her husband promised to be faithful to her.

Then came their eighth wedding anniversary. When Hall went to work in the morning he told his wife he wouldn't be home 'til teatime, because he had to go to the Temple. He kissed her good-bye and went off. She worked, happy as a lark; this was the happiest day since they had left New York. She tidied up the garden and cleaned the house so that everything would look nice to her husband when he came home. In the afternoon she was arranging some wildflowers she had picked when their dog, Tiger, started barking outside. She thought it was strangers and went to the door. Her husband was coming down the path with a strange woman hanging on his arm, bold as brass. They walked past her as if she hadn't been there and went into the house.

"I have been sealed in spirit to this woman today," Hall said. "I expect you to welcome her and show her respect."

The other woman made herself at home and looked about the place.

"Looks like you was expecting me," she simpered. "House seems pretty well fixed up, but she doesn't seem to be glad. We'll make her know I'm mistress here now, won't we, Mr. Hall?"

The poor woman was heartbroken.

She stuck it out for a few days but her husband didn't have eyes for anyone but his new wife. Mrs. Hall ran away. She went to Font Lake where the Mormons baptized converts and Tiger, the dog, followed her. Twice she tried to throw herself into the water but that faithful dog held on to her skirt and saved her life. For days she wandered through the woods, she and the dog, almost starving.

108

A day or so later Hall went out and shot that poor, faithful dog who hadn't done anything but save the woman's life. Her sister and brother-in-law finally found her and took her to the mainland where they escaped from King James. They told all the people who'd listen about the goings on on the island, about this man who set himself up as king, even higher than the President. They went to the Governor in Lansing, then to Detroit to tell the Federal judge.

In May, 1851, the Government sent the U.S.S. Michigan, that was the ship that brought my parents and me to the island, to see what was going on. They arrested the king and forty of his elders and apostles on charges of counterfeiting, piracy, interfering with the mails, theft from Federal mail and a dozen other things, including murder! They let most of them go except Strang, Adams and a few higher ups and those they took to the United States District Court at Detroit.

For twenty days Strang defended himself; he had a counsel, but he figured that he was a good enough lawyer to look after his own defense. He wore his black suit and stove pipe hat and Adams stood around looking like a cigar store Indian in his actor's robes; he said they were the same he had worn on the Boston stage and in the Temple services at Voree.

Well, sir, Strang denied that he had ordered Bennet's killing or that Mormons had done it. He said there were no pirates sailing out of Beaver Island. He talked to that jury and his tongue was like silver. And that jury believed him and said "Not Guilty" to all charges against him.

King James came back to Beaver Island more full of himself than ever; even the U.S. Government couldn't beat him. He planned to take over the whole of Northern Michigan, and in the Fall elections his people had every office in Mackinac County and that included all the courts. The county seat was moved to Beaver Island where King James could keep his eye on everything. The next year he was in the State Legislature and served two terms. Everybody was flabbergasted, but there it was. The man who said he was a king was actually in a State Legislature of the United States. The Detroit Advertiser said at the time (I kept the clipping): *"Whatever may be said or thought of the peculiar sect of which he is the local head, throughout this session he has conducted himself with a degree of decorum and propriety which have been equaled by his industry, sagacity, good temper, apparent regard for the true interests of the people and the obligations of his official oath."*

For four years after his trial, he reigned as king of Beaver Island. He started a newspaper, the Northern Islander, and edited it himself.

Some of his people tried to escape from the island but they were brought back and flogged nearly to death, and woes betide those who tried to help them. Every week he'd get new revelations that would mean new laws and fancy ways to drag more money out of his people. He wouldn't take advice from any man. I believe he thought he was as mighty as the Lord Himself! It was in 1856 that he passed the law that fixed him

110

good. At that time a Mrs. Bloomer of New York State was preaching about women wearing pants the same as men. They were more practical, she said, and more healthy, too.

Quaint Old Cartoon That Appeared in the French Magazine, "La Caricature," Poking Fun at the Bloomer Fad — But "King" Strang Didn't Think the Fashion Was Funny. (From the Bettmann Archives.)

King James heard about it and he wanted to be the first one in any new fangled idea so he passed a law saying that all the women in his kingdom must wear those pantaloons. Well sir, that made them madder than the celestial marriage law did. In those days women wore skirts down to their boots, and those who showed as much as an ankle were the lost ones.

The women gabbled and chatted about the town; they weren't going to wear any brazen garments like those, they said. And the two families who made the most fuss were the Alexander Wentworths and the Thomas Bedfords.

When Strang ordered all the women to come to his "royal court" in bloomers, one of the ladies---I don't remember whether it was Mrs. Wentworth or Mrs. Bedford---flatly refused to go, and the other swished right into the "royal" presence wearing forbidden skirts.

So the Wentworths and the Bedfords were arrested by Strang's plug-uglies and the four of them, women, too, were given 75 strokes with the "blue beeches".

The husbands swore they'd get even, and Bedford said right out loud that he'd kill the king.

Right in the middle of the bloomer trouble, Strang ordered all gentiles to get off the island and gave them ten days to do it in. My family had already left and we were living on the mainland near Pine River. The order said that "all gentiles must move out or go to the Temple to be baptized into the Church of Zion". The fishermen packed up pronto and set sail for the mainland. But they took with them two Mormon families who had been trying to escape from Strang for months. King James heard that they were staying with fishermen on the mainland, and he sent two boatloads of armed thugs to bring them back, dead or alive.

Did you ever hear of the Battle of Pine River? Well, I'm the only (last) survivor of it. I saw that battle from beginning to end, and here's how it went:

A few days after the fishermen left the island and settled on the mainland, they were fishing in the lake when they sighted the two boatloads of Strang's men. They put on sail and managed to reach the shore before Strang's men and hid themselves and the refugees in the woods until the thugs should go away. The thugs landed and were met by Captain Morrison and Louis

Geebo (Gebeau), who were mainlanders. I was still only a small kid, but I hung about Geebo waiting to see what would happen. They were a big crowd, all whiskers and black hats and every one of them had a gun or revolver. They demanded that the two Mormon families give themselves up. But Captain Morrison wasn't scared of 'em.

"No sir," he said. "They've chose to live with us and we aim to protect them".

They argued and confabbed for a long time, me dodging about their legs and listening with all my ears, but Morrison was mighty peart (pert) and wouldn't make any promises. Then the leader of the gang jerked his head, spat, and the mob turned to go back to their boats. Just as they reached the beach they turned round and started shooting.

I dropped on my face, scared as a rabbit while bullets clipped the bushes all about us. Geebo was standing near and I grabbed his leg, feeling better to have something human to hold on to. They were shouting and firing, and suddenly Geebo let out a curse and drops right on top of me. There was blood on my face where a bullet smashed his knee. Why that bullet didn't kill me I don't know, for it went through his knee not an inch from my head.

Geebo yelled and the fishermen started dodging out of the woods, mad as wolves. They had fish gigs and oars and there were a few rifles and pistols. Strang's men weren't so brave when they saw armed men after them, so they jumped into their boats and started rowing out into the lake.

"Let 'em go," yelled the women.

But the fishermen were blazing mad that one of their men had been shot and started in their boats after them. I was sitting up beside Louis Geboo, watching, and it looked like one of those ancient sea battles in history. For half an hour rifles and pistols banged across the lake with puffs of smoke where the guns went off and the boats rowed farther and farther from shore. I could hear the fishermen cursing and Strang's men yelling back.

Then one of Strang's boats started sinking and there was a mighty yell from our side. Some were wounded, I could hear them praying and crying out and more than one was dead, hanging over the side of the boat with his head in the water. The other boat dragged Strang's men out of the sinking craft and there was a shout as the Barque Morgan, veered through the mist. Strang's crowd managed to get aboard her and the fishermen pulled alongside daring them to come down and fight.

But the Barque took Strang's men back to the island and the fishermen came ashore where their wives were waiting mighty anxious. They felt better when they learned that the only one hurt was poor Louis Geboo and he was cussing a blue streak while they bandaged his knee.

That stopped Strang interfering with the mainland. Although Strang's paper printed a story of the battle where he said that his men had been attacked and seven killed and five wounded.

But Wentworth and Bedford had a bone to pick with the red headed little terror. They begged Dr. McCullough, the doctor on Beaver Island, to help them get rid of the king. He said he wouldn't take a hand in killing a man, but he would try and bring the law to Beaver Island.

He told King James he had to go to the mainland for medical supplies and to see other doctors about a cure for cholera which had killed off a lot of people the previous Summer. Strang let him go and he went straight to the State capital at Lansing. There he told Governor Bingham the whole story and said he'd have to take action because men and women were being treated like slaves by the king.

The Governor listened and made his mind up quickly. He went to Detroit and argued with the Federal Government until they sent the Michigan to the island again. This time there was a company of Marines aboard.

Strang was ordered to give himself up for questioning. At first he refused, but was told that if he didn't go aboard the ship, the Marines would come and get him. Well, the Marines were too much even for Strang and he agreed to go.

The little man, red hair sticking out from under his chimney pot hat walked along the wharf to board the Michigan. But he didn't see Bedford and Wentworth hiding behind some stacks of cordwood. They waited until he was abreast of them, then jumped out, shooting.

Both bullets hit Strang and he dropped!

Wentworth and Bedford bolted for the Michigan to give themselves up before Strang's men could catch them. Strang, lying on the deck managed to grab their legs, but they smashed him over the head with their pistol butts and got away to the Marines. They were taken to Mackinaw City and the people cheered like they were heroes.

But by U.S. law they had to be locked up in jail. They stayed there a week. Then one night they heard their cell door open by a man they'd never seen before.

"Don't ask questions," he whispered. "Run to the dock and get aboard the steamer."

They ran for it and escaped. They lived out their lives near Charlevoix, quite openly with their families, and were never rearrested nor brought to trial.

And while they were escaping, Strang was dying. He lived eleven days after the shooting, cared for by four wives, a nurse and Doctor McCullough.

But now, near death, he began to think of all the bad things he'd done; he started thinking of his faithful wife whom he'd deserted for the four other wives. He begged the doctor to take him to Burlington to spend his last hours with her. McCullough consented and Strang sent for his apostles to give them his orders as how to rule the island after he was dead and gone. They took him to Burlington and his wife—after all he

116

did to her—forgave him!

She nursed him for a few days and on June 9th, 1856, he died in her arms. He was only forty-three and had lived as full a life as most men double his age; almost as full as mine.

But after he was buried the people on Beaver Island weren't taking another king. They wouldn't even obey the leaders. Some of the plug-uglies who had flogged many a good man and woman were bushwhacked in quiet lanes and given a taste of their own medicine. And by now the gentiles who had been driven off the island started coming back to claim their own. They weren't having another King James Strang. But they couldn't get help from the Government, so they banded together on their own.

They got a tremendous mob and commandeered two lake steamers, the Keystone State and the Iowa. They got guns and swords, and landed on Beaver Island.

First thing they did was to burn the tabernacle. Then they burned shops and houses. They took back the things Strang had taken from them, and plenty more besides. And all of Strang's men they caught and drove with their children aboard the two steamers. They were set ashore in Chicago a few days later; homeless, hungry, tired, they were left to roam the Midwest to make out as best they could.

The fishermen took over the island. Some lived in old

houses, others built new ones. Today the water around Beaver Island is still the best fishing ground in Lake Michigan. I know it, for often these days I take a small boat and sit there in the sun wetting a line and catching many a good lake trout. Sometimes I think of the times when King Strang was emperor of the island and the lake, and I was a pop-eyed little shaver scared to death of him.

But I lasted him out.

Yes, sir, I'm an old man now, the only one living who saw King Strang. I'm going to my account soon, but I'm glad I don't have to answer for the things he did. No, sir!

Stephen H. Smith
1922

Appendix B

Murderous Assault
From the Daily Northern Islander
An Account of the shooting of
"King" Jesse James Strang

This story appeared on the front page of the issue of the Daily Northern Islander *dated Friday, June 20, 1856. It gives details of the shooting of Strang in a surprisingly dispassionate account.*

On Monday last the U.S. steamer Michigan entered this harbour at about 1 o'clock, P.M., and was visited by the inhabitants promiscuously during the afternoon.

At about 7 o'clock Capt. McBlair sent a messenger (San Bernard, the Pilot) to Mr. Strang, requesting him to visit him on board. Mr. Strang immediately accompanied the messenger, and just as they were stepping on the bridge leading to the pier in front of F. Johnson & Co.'s store, two assassins approached in the rear, unobserved by either of them, and fired upon Mr. Strang with pistols. The first shot took effect upon the left side of the head, entering a little back of the top of the ear, and rebounding, passed out near the top of the head.

This shot, fired from a horse pistol, brought him down, and he fell on the left side, so that he saw the assassins as they fired the second and third shots from a revolver; both taking effect upon his person, one just below the

119

temple, on the right side of the face, and lodged in the cheek bone; the other on the left side of the spine, near the tenth rib, followed the rib about two inches and a half and lodged. Mr. Strang recognized in the persons of the assassins Thomas Bedford and Alexander Wentworth. Wentworth had a revolver, and Bedford a horse pistol, with which he struck him over the head and face, while lying on the ground. The assassins immediately fled on board the U.S. steamer, with pistols in hand, claiming her protection. The assault was committed in view of several of the officers and crew from the deck of the steamer, also Dr. H.D. McCulloch, Franklin Johnson, and others, and no effort made to stop it.

Mr. Strang was taken up by a few friends, and some of the officers of the boat, and carried to the house of Messrs. Prindles, where the surgeon of the steamer made an examination of his wounds, and declared recovery hopeless.

Process was taken out for the apprehension of the assassins, and the Sheriff of the county called on Capt. McBlair for their delivery. The Capt. refused to give them up, saying that he would take them to Mackinac, and deliver them into the hands of the civil authorities of the State there.

The steamer left the next day, carrying off all the persons supposed to be complicated in the affair, thus affording military protection to murderers, and overthrowing the sovereignty of civil law.

Hopes are entertained of Mr. Strang's recovery.

Further down the page, this announcement was made:

In consequence of the laying up of Mr. Strang with his wounds, and the disarrangement of affairs growing out of the occurrence, the Daily Islander will be suspended.

Appendix C

The Battle of Pine River
The Mystery of Its Date

By Audrey S. Hilliker, granddaughter of Stephen H. Smith

In 1922, my grandfather, Stephen H. Smith, of Charlevoix, Michigan, finished an autobiographical account of his early days, beginning in 1852 when, at the age of three years, he moved to northern Michigan with his parents, Thomas and Phebe Smith. He takes the narrative through 1864, when his father began to farm on a homestead claim in Marion Township.

In the first chapter of his book, Grandfather says that some subjects which have been touched upon by other writers "are innocently incorrect and in some cases have been purposely distorted and willfully falsified". I am sure that he felt that the date of the Battle of Pine River was one of the items falsified. But the question might be asked: why would anyone want to falsify this date?

I have heard Grandfather tell the story many times of his participation in the Battle of Pine River. I do not doubt that it really happened, and that it made an indelible impression on him. He was a very honest, conscientious person, and I cannot believe that he simply made up the story. So I am going to proceed on the assumption that the story is true, and trust that the correct date will unfold as we go along.

The first mention of the Battle of Pine River by this name occurred in the book "The Traverse Region, Historical and Descriptive" by H.R. Page & Co., published in 1884. This was also the first book to give it a date— July 13, 1853. Others who wrote later seem to have simply accepted this date without question, so what might seem to be a preponderance of evidence as to its correctness could simply result from the pyramiding effect of each author's copying an earlier source. It is important, therefore, to ascertain whether this earlier source was completely reliable.

The earlier source used by Mr. Page seems to be the newspaper, Detroit Daily Advertiser, but the copy from which he quotes the story of the battle is undated. A search in the Burton Historical Collection in the Detroit Public Library of the bound volume containing this newspaper for 1853, focusing especially on the seven days beginning July 14, 1853, does not reveal this story, which was supposedly written by James J. Strang.

On July 21, 1853, there was an article "The Mormon Affair" which was reprinted from The Chicago Journal of Monday, July 18, 1853, written by the captain of the Barque Morgan. To confuse the issue further, this gave the date of the battle as July 13, 1852!

It is of interest to find, also, that copies of the Detroit Daily Advertiser between 1841 and 1857 are missing from the State Library in Lansing, Michigan.

Before the publication of the book by Page, there had been two other books which reported on this battle, neither of which gave it a name or a date. The so-called Mormon version was contained in a 48 page pamphlet entitled "Ancient and Modern Michilimackinac, including an account of the Controversy between Mackinac and the Mormons". It was also written by James J. Strang and printed at St. James, Michigan in 1854.

According to information contained in a copy of this edition made later, this pamphlet was based upon a series of articles entitled "Beaver Island and Emmet County" which ran in the newspaper "Northern Islander" once a month – in January, February, March and April, 1854.

This newspaper was also printed at St. James, with much of its material written by Mr. Strang, and ran intermittently. According to records in the Detroit Public Library, "there was no issue of the Northern Islander for July 14, 1853." However, I was able to obtain a photocopy of the Photostat of the so-called "Extra" of that date from the Curator of the Western Americana Collection at Yale University.

According to the Beaver Island Historical Society Library, their collection of the Northern Islander Newspaper has a gap from June, 1853 to July, 1854, which would include the so-called "Extra" as well as the series on Beaver Island and Emmet County mentioned above.

Even though there was supposed to have been this "Extra" Edition of the Northern Islander on July 14, 1853, strangely enough, Mr. Strang, writing his pamphlet in

1854, does not mention it or quote from it or give the battle a date based on it. This might lead one to believe that the battle had actually occurred quite recently, but any attempt to date it further into the past had not yet been made.

In this latter pamphlet, the Pine River story appears under the heading "EFFORT TO OVERRIDE THE LIQUOR LAW IN EMMET", part of the continuing attempts to picture the fishermen at Pine River as a group of unscrupulous outlaws, benefiting from selling bad whiskey to the Indians.

But the tactics were evidently changed, and the pamphlet goes on to state that the Sheriff of Emmet County, who was at that time based on Beaver Island, went to Pine River taking two boats and fourteen men, supposedly unarmed, to summon three men residing there to serve as Jurors for the approaching Circuit Court. They were met by between sixty and eighty men, it relates, were fired upon and pursued for twelve miles before being rescued by the Barque Morgan.

This Northern Islander Extra mentioned above was included, word for word, (but not in newspaper format) in a pamphlet published some time after April 3, 1892. (It contained an article by Mr. Strang's son of that date, as well as a report on the death of King Strang.) Grandfather had a copy of this pamphlet and also the one on "Ancient and Modern Michilimackinac" by Mr. Strang.

The "Extra" account in the later pamphlet adds a few details to Mr. Strang's version. While still claiming that the men were unarmed, it was admitted that there were four guns in the bottom of one of the boats, which, however, "were not taken up nor seen by any one while at Pine River". The number of men who met them was variously reported as 30, 50, or 60 with 200 guns! The number of boatloads of men who pursued them was given as three.

We must remember that all of the above material included in the Mormon version itself and the two questionable newspaper accounts were written by James J. Strang, a man who had been accused of using a forged letter from the Mormon leader, Joseph Smith, as justification for his claim to be Smith's successor. He was also a man who had access to his own printing press! Is it not possible that the two newspaper accounts were "planted" to serve his own purposes, and were not necessarily printed on the dates it was claimed that they were?

The so-called "gentile" version, which appeared the year before the Page book (1883), was "History of the Grand Traverse Region" by Dr. M.L. Leach. This was first printed in the newspaper, "Grand Traverse Herald", Traverse City, Michigan, in that year. Mr. Page had drawn heavily on Dr. Leach's book, quoting some of it verbatim, as did some other writers who came later.

Although the skirmish had taken place at least twenty-seven years before, Dr. Leach refers to it only as "A Battle" and gives no date. He makes two references to my great-grandfather, Thomas Smith, and two to his brother, T.D. Smith. According to Dr. Leach there were two Mormons named Hull and Savage, who had escaped from Beaver Island and asked the protection of the mainland fishermen. There was also a fisherman named Moon, whom the Mormons were anxious to arrest. So two boats set out, containing eighteen men, which constituted an "armed party, accompanied by an officer, with a subpoena for the three men". He suggests it may have been tied in with the meeting of the Circuit Court, to make it appear more legal.

He first introduces the idea that the women of the community were gathered for a quilting bee at the home of Captain Morrison, and quotes the famous "wade in blood" speech, which in turn is a quote from a former remark made by King Strang, to the effect that they would wade in blood up to their ankles if necessary to establish their dominion.

He also mentions the shooting in the leg of one of the young fishermen named Lewis Gebeau, which he misspells as "Geboo". According to his account, Geboo had lived on Beaver Island (which is true) and recognized some of his former acquaintances. Thinking the confrontation was over, he started to walk down to talk with them, then decided it was only prudent to check his gun. When he did so, he was shot in the leg by one of the frustrated Mormon leaders, Jonathan Pierce.

This account by Dr. Leach says there was only one boat which pursued the Mormons, but agrees with the Mormon account of the rescue by the Barque Morgan. All gentile accounts seem to agree that the families at Pine River left soon after, at least temporarily, Dr. Leach supplying the detail that the steamer Columbia came in and took them to their various destinations.

Elizabeth Whitney Williams, whose book "A Child of the Sea; and Life Among the Mormons" was published in 1905, quotes much of the Leach version verbatim including the reason for the Mormons' visit as being the desire to arrest three men who were Mormon enemies. She accepts the Page date – July 13, 1853 -- but refers to it as the Battle at Charlevoix.

She claims that as a child she was watching from a window in the Morrison's home when the boats came ashore, and that her father, Walter Whitney, and later Captain Morrison, spoke to the Mormons. She says that Captain Morrison's boat was the only one which pursued the Mormons when they left. She corrects the spelling of the name, Lewis Geboo, to Lewis Gebeau, who, after all, was her half-brother, so she ought to know! She confirms that he was shot in the leg, but makes no comment on the reason given by Leach as leading up to it.

So now we come to Grandfather's account. Grandfather says that the "skirmish" took place in the spring of 1856. He maintains that there were three boatloads of Mormons facing between 26 and 28 fishermen on the mainland, agrees that the Mormons were rescued by the Barque Morgan, and that the settlers left Pine River shortly afterward. He places the quilting bee at the Savage home, and has one of the frightened women confronting the Mormons, and hearing the "wade in blood" speech. He—a little boy of seven—was clinging tightly to the pant leg of Lewis Gebeau (since his father had placed him in the care of Gebeau, who was one of his hired men) when the same leg was shot.

In addition to Lewis Gebeau and himself, Grandfather mentions two other people as being involved in the battle—his father, Tom Smith, and his uncle, Tim (T.D.) Smith. If the battle took place in July, 1853, he and his father could not have been a part of it. His own record is substantiated by a rather derogatory reference to his father, Tom, in the Northern Islander newspaper of June 30, 1853, which places him as keeper of the lighthouse at Beaver Island "last winter" but as the present keeper of the light on "Isle Le Galet" (Skille gul les).

Grandfather mentions that Uncle Tim came to visit them at Skille gul les in the late summer (blackberry season) of 1853. If there had been a battle in July, wouldn't Tim, who hated to miss any excitement, have been full of the news of it? And wouldn't little Stephen have been right there, drinking in every word of it? (Although only sixteen years his senior, Uncle Tim was a sort of a folk hero to Stephen.)

The two dates that Grandfather gives as confirming his own remembrance that the battle occurred in 1856 have been independently verified from family records. These were the wedding of Uncle Tim on January 14 and the birth of Grandfather's sister on February 18 of that year.

In order to be completely fair and subject Grandfather's claim to the same scrutiny given the 1853 date, I have asked myself "Could there have been other events, equally frightening, which occurred in other years and were combined in memory with the Battle of Pine River?"

We know that the period between 1853 and 1856 was one of almost continual turmoil between the Mormons and the mainland fishermen. The Northern Islander newspaper of December 6, 1855, refers to the men of Mackinac (which, no doubt, includes other fishermen nearer by) as having "been engaged in bitter hostility against the Mormons for six years, and have several times been engaged in bloody conflicts against them."

The year 1855 included the harassing of the John Dixon family, who were trying to locate at Pine River, and the burning of the Smith's cooper shop at Middle Village. Of this, Dr. Leach has this to say: "About two weeks after the departure of the (Dixon) party for Northport, Capt. T.D. Smith and his brother, Thomas, arrived at Pine River from Middle Village, having come for the purpose of rendering any assistance Mr. Dixon might need in his conflict with the Mormons. Some months before, the Mormons had burned the cooper shop at Middle Village belonging to the Smiths; they were therefore prepared to take advantage of any opportunity to avenge their own wrongs while assisting others."

This trip taken by her husband, Thomas, certainly might have been an anxious time for the young mother, left alone with two children, including a baby daughter born January 12 of that year. (This daughter did not survive until the 1860 census. Another daughter was born in February, 1856.)

What about Uncle Tim, married in January, 1856? While he could very well have been in the Battle of

Footprints in the Sand

Pine River, it is also possible he took part in the clearing of the Mormons from Beaver Island in the summer of 1856. (Grandfather implies that his father was not involved in it, but he doesn't mention Tim, one way or the other.) Could this have been the event mentioned by Grandfather in his story when Tim left his young bride to participate in a dangerous activity?

Grandfather's account of the celebration at Cross Village, July 4, 1855, shows that it was at least partly devoted to consideration of the Mormon menace, and that the fishermen in attendance had resolved that if appeals to State and Federal Governments were unavailing, they would take matters into their hands the next year.

That this resolution was being carried out is indicated in a report in the Livingston Courier under the heading "The Mormons of Beaver Island". It transmitted a long letter dated "Grand Traverse, Mich. Sept. 10, 1855" which outlined the many difficulties being encountered by John S. Dixon at Pine River, and concludes: "The facts communicated, it seems to us, call loudly upon both State and National governments to interfere for the defense and protection of the hardy settlers who have made their homes around Grand Traverse Bay. We hope the Press of the State will generally copy the letter. –Livingston Courier"

Another meeting, also in July, 1855, was the one held by the Mormons at Holy Island in the South Arm of Pine Lake (later Lake Charlevoix). According to the book "Bob Miles' Charlevoix", although it was publicly proclaimed as a giving of thanks to the Almighty, "The

131

real business at hand was to formulate plans for the rapid settlement of the mainland by the Mormons to the exclusion of the Gentiles. Lands were acquired through Strang's political stranglehold (as a member of the State legislature, to which he had won re-election in 1854) and by autumn three boats were employed between Beaver Island and the mainland, bringing a steady stream of immigrants."

I do not put it beyond the range of possibility that at some time in the next few months the mainland settlers might have challenged those "three boats". Remember, Grandfather referred to three boats in his account, and he doesn't mention enforcing the whiskey laws, summoning jurors, or retaking men as the reason for the Mormons' visit.

If there was, indeed, another confrontation in the spring of 1856, it is possible it was overshadowed by the dramatic events which followed in close succession—the assassination of King Strang in June, his death on July 9, and the driving out of the Mormons from Beaver Island that same summer. Possibly, as time went on, these might have been combined in thought with memories of an earlier battle; but a confrontation in the spring of 1856 might also have had a bearing on bringing those final events to a head.

Let us now examine still a third possibility. Could the battle possibly have taken place in the spring of 1854? The little family had left Skille gul les in the fall of 1853, spent the winter at Little Traverse (now Harbor Springs), and moved to Pine River for the spring fishing, even going so far as to build a rough shelter there.

So as far as they were concerned, the battle probably could have taken place that year.

Now let us go back to Mr. Strang and his pamphlet "Ancient and Modern Michilimackinac", the part pertaining to this subject having been reprinted from the Daily Northern Islander newspaper of April 13, 1854.

After discussion of the confrontation which took place between the Mormon visitors and the mainland fishermen (no date given) it says: "The intention of the outlaws was to kill the whole party, and then report that they had been killed while engaged in committing some crime, and thus set public indignation against the Mormons. The sheriff escaping, they took alarm, lest some single act of revenge should follow, and all fled. + + + + Scattering in such hot haste, they failed to agree upon any story to tell, for the purpose of charging the blame on the Mormons. At Mackinac an attempt was made to put afloat the story that the Mormons had shot first, and wounded a boy. But the history of the matter was already before the public, and they failed to successfully falsify it."

In this mention of the wounding of "a boy", Mr. Strang is getting into the so-called gentile accounts. Almost every gentile account included this story, some giving "the boy" a name and others not. So, in spite of attempts to squelch the story it continued to grow.

The most modern reprint of the pamphlet (1894) says: "Strang's purpose in publishing the book was to present the Mormon side of the conflict with the inhabitants of Mackinac and the other gentiles of the area.

This is a political, not a religious tract."

In 1854, James J. Strang was running for re-election to the State Legislature. He was trying to portray the Mormon colony as the victim, not the aggressor. But here was this Lewis Gebeau, a living witness to the fact that the Mormons, who supposedly were unarmed, fired the first shot and perhaps brought upon themselves the treatment they received. (He was evidently not familiar with Grandfather's mention of the stuttering Mr. Going, which might have given them an alibi, but remember, Grandfather is only five years old at this time!)

Was he perhaps tempted to move the battle back to the summer before, even to the extent of getting out a couple of phony newspaper accounts, in which any mention of a boy's being wounded are carefully avoided? While he might not be able to fool those of his constituents who lived nearby, whose votes he probably wouldn't get anyway, most of them lived far away from this wilderness area which he was hoping so desperately to settle with Mormons. We will probably never know for sure, and yet, things do have a way of coming to the surface sometimes.

"The King Strang Story" by Doyle Fitzpatrick says (page 108): "A year after this July, 1853 battle, a situation developed between the new Pine River Gentile settlers and a small number of Mormon settlers, similar to the feud between Mackinac and Beaver. The Pine River settlement became firmly established at this time and marked the beginning of Mormon expansion in that area."

This at least opens up the possibility that the battle could have been in 1854, and also confirms the Mormon expansion in which Strang was engaged, which he so desperately wanted to perpetuate by remaining in the Legislature.

So, to summarize: proceeding on the premise that Grandfather as a young child was a participant in the battle which was later called the "Battle of Pine River", we arrive at the conclusions: (1) that it could not have occurred in July, 1853, when he and his family were living in a very isolated spot; (2) that it really could have occurred in 1856, when Grandfather says it did, as part of the several confrontations between Mormons and mainlanders during that period in history, but might have been combined in memory with an earlier battle or with other dramatic events of that same year and (3) that that earlier battle—if there was one—might have occurred in the spring of 1854, when the family was temporarily living in Pine River.

In the later case, the establishment of a falsified date of July, 1853, required some manipulation by a man who was quite adept at such things, and who possibly felt he could win another term in the legislature if the turmoil of the region were relegated further into the past, something he desperately wanted in order to facilitate the continued Mormon colonization of the mainland.

What difference does the date make, especially after all these years? Probably none, to the average person, but I am sure it did to my grandfather, who wanted very much to be judged in the annals of history as a truthful person and a trustworthy historian.

Looking back at the struggles which characterized this early settlement of northern Michigan, one is inclined to remember the pioneer days of the West, when there were petty wars between the farmers and the ranchers. Finally, though, they learned to live together in peace. But just as the Mormons had pushed out the Gentiles from Beaver Island in 1852, they were themselves dispersed in 1856, and the opportunity to live and grow and settle in the land together was forever lost.

Audrey S. Hilliker
1985

Appendix D
*Story in Grand Rapids Press
Printed Summer of 1940*

Only Living Witness

"Stephen H. Smith, 91, to Uncover Stone Marking Battle of Pine River"

Text on the marker reads: Battle of "Pine River" was fought on this site the evening of July 13, 1853 between a party of Mormons from Beaver Island and fishermen settlers of the new settlement of Pine River later named Charlevoix in 1879.

Charlevoix--- You may have forgotten there was such a battle, or never known it, but a monument marking the site of the battle of Pine River will be dedicated here Saturday.

Stephen H. Smith, who at 91 is one of the region's oldest pioneers and the only living witness of the battle, will uncover the big native stone bearing a bronze plaque that records the event.

The battlefield on the shore of Lake Michigan was virgin wilderness when mainland fishermen engaged "King" James J. Strang of Beaver Island and his colonists in June of 1856. (Editor's Note: The true date is and always will be a mystery.)

When he was 3 years old, Smith's father was keeper of the lighthouse at the head of Beaver Island and the "king" of the colony was a frequent visitor in their home. Later, in 1854, the Smiths went to Pine River, now Charlevoix, and were believed to be the first white colonists at this point on the mainland.

On July 4, 1855 at Cross Village, the fighting men of the mainland assembled to formulate plans to stop depredations attributed to the island colonists. At that time, boats, cargoes and even crews were disappearing with alarming regularity. Nets of fishermen who depended upon them for their livelihood were being stolen and burned.

The next year, when Stephen was 7 years old, a group of the islanders walked into an ambush prepared by the mainland fisherfolk. In the ensuing battle, many of the islanders were wounded and all were driven from the mainland.

Six weeks after the Pine River battle, someone killed "King" Strang and the war between the mainlanders and the islanders was over.

Appendix E
*Reprinted from Grand Rapids Press with Photo
Friday, August 22, 1941*

Charlevoix Pioneer Dies
"Pine River" Battle Witness, Steve Smith, Taken by Death

Charlevoix—Stephen H. Smith, 92, one of northern Michigan's pioneers and a resident of Beaver Island in the reign of the "king," James J. Strang, died here Thursday. Smith is believed to have been the last surviving eye-witness of the historic battle of Pine River between the Mormons and the mainland fishermen.

Mr. Smith, born at Redford in 1849, was taken to Beaver Island at the age of 3 when his father, Thomas, was appointed lightkeeper there. The isle was then occupied by the Mormon colony. Before Smith's family was driven off the isle because of a refusal to join the

Mormons, "King" Strang had been a frequent visitor at their home.

Strife Arises.

Mr. Smith also witnessed the first Fourth of July celebration ever held in northern Michigan, the fete being held at Cross Village in 1855. Purpose of the gathering, at which 200 persons attended, was not so much to celebrate Independence Day as to make plans to combat Mormon depredations. At the time, fishing boats and their crews were "disappearing".

The trouble came to a violent climax in 1856 when, in June, the historic Pine River battle was fought at a point on Lake Michigan near the present coast guard station. Smith, a boy then, was an eye-witness as fishermen, seeing Mormon boats approaching, concealed themselves in the woods. The Mormons landed and went to a home where the fishermen's wives were holding a quilting bee and threatened to kill the husbands. As they made the threat, the fishermen opened fire, wounded the Mormons and drove them off.

Smith, only 7, found himself sheltered behind Louis Gebeau when the shooting started. In the exchange of gunshots, a bullet wounded Gebeau on the knee of the leg Smith was clinging to. Six weeks after the battle, "King" Strang was killed and the "war" terminated.

Fled from Isle.

In 1854 the Smiths, having left the island, came to Pine River, now Charlevoix, and were believed to be the first white colonists at this point on the mainland.

In 1864 Mr. Smith cut the first trail from Lake Michigan's shore into the wilderness to a location in what is now Marion Township, and with his parents homesteaded there. He resided there until 27 years ago. (when he moved into town in Charlevoix. Editor's note.)

Mr. Smith had written a history of northern Michigan. Surviving are a daughter, Mrs. Arthur Staley at whose home he died; a brother, Frank Smith of Bellaire, and a sister, Mrs. Mary McFarland of Charlevoix.

Epilogue

The Rest of the Story.....

by Donna L. Staley Heeres
Great Granddaughter of Stephen H. Smith

My great grandfather's story ends in 1860. Obviously, there was more to his life after he turned 11 years of age. Even his story that was published in the American Weekly on September 1, 1940, centers upon the early years of his life. To be sure, the first years of his life had a profound impact on him.

During my childhood, I often heard anecdotes about Grandpa Stevie as he was lovingly referred to. My earliest memories were of a picture taken of him, near the end of his life, and obviously before the beginning of mine. He was seated in a straight chair, out in the yard, with his daughter (my grandmother) Mildred Smith Staley and his grand daughter (my aunt) Dorothy Staley Richards. His great grandson Lynn Richards was a small child in this picture, thus making it a four generations photo. He had a large white mustache and was dressed in a dark suit. This photo was taken in the side yard at 401 Antrim where the grocery store was located and where my parents still live.

Other stories include his wife, Hattie. It seems that Grandpa Stevie had a vision problem and Grandma Hattie had a hearing problem. References were often made to Grandpa trying to find the butter on the table and rather loudly and emphatically asking Grandma Hattie to pass the "BUTTER, HATTIE, BUTTER!" I am sure the reader does not get the humor in this, but I know my family will all smile at this recollection as we all have for much of our lives!

Grandpa Stevie's obituary refers to the homesteading of property in 1864 in what is now Marion Township. Other records show that Stephen's grandfather, William Smith, along with his father Thomas, had staked a homestead claim in that same area south of Charlevoix. These farms are located on Marion Center Road, north of Black Road. Other stories are passed down about an ongoing battle between my great great grandfather Thomas Smith who homesteaded the farm and a neighbor. Apparently, the water supply for the cattle on the two neighboring farms was sparse. The neighbors both needed water for their cattle and from time to time each would divert the supply to their own cattle. There was a battle that ended up with the neighbor being shot and Thomas being sent to Jackson Prison. However, the prosecutor decided that Thomas was imprisoned on circumstantial evidence and before the prosecutor retired, Thomas was exonerated. He died a short time after he was released from prison.

In September of 1869, the Charlevoix Sentinel newspaper, reported that "S.S. Liscomb would notify the public that he has permanently located at the village of Charlevoix and will do all kinds of repairing of watches, clocks, etc. Work can be left either at the Fountain City House or at the store of A. Buttars & Co." S.S. Liscomb's daughter, Hattie, would later meet and marry Stephen Smith.

In February 1877, The Charlevoix Sentinel (newspaper) reported that "Stephen H. Smith of Marion has entered into a partnership with Sam'l Rounsville, an experienced nurseryman of Wisconsin and will, the coming spring, transplant a large quantity of setts upon his place with the view of establishing a permanent nursery. It is good philosophy that trees climatized here will be much more thrifty than stock imported from other climates." In April of the same year, the same newspaper reported "Judge drawn for the May term of the circuit court for Charlevoix County from Marion was Stephen Smith."

Grandpa Stevie and Grandma Hattie were married November 29, 1877 in Charlevoix. The Charlevoix Sentinel reported it thusly on December 4, 1877: " Married. Another of the famed and nearly extinct family of Smith's has consigned himself to the everlasting blessedness of matrimony. Stephen H is the victim this time and Miss Hattie Liscomb, daughter of S.S. Liscomb of this place was the bride. She cannot but be happy with one of the name of Smith and he has in the person of Hattie an estimable wife. Long life and happiness with plenty of buckwheat cakes and molasses is the wish of the editor."

They raised four children, the youngest being my grandmother Mildred Smith (1888-1949). Other children included Gertrude (1878-1929), Jessie (1880-1882) and Stephen Milo (1882-1905).

Grandpa Stevie raised large and small fruits on the farm. He was state agent for Runyan Standard Lock Fence. He was a Mason for 34 years. About 1919, when Grandpa Stevie was 70 years old, he and Grandma Hattie purchased the neighborhood grocery store from the original owner/builder, the Crandalls. He should have been retiring, but he purchased a grocery store! Mr. Crandall had moved counters and windows from a store in Cross Village into Charlevoix. At the time the grocery store was built, it was located along US 31. The route formerly crossed the bridge and followed the shore of Round Lake to what is now Antrim Street. The highway then turned west to Sheridan Street, then south, crossing what is now the airport, connecting to Barnard Road to Norwood, then south on Old Dixie Highway to Eastport and Traverse City. The store was on a main thoroughfare through Charlevoix and prospered there for many years! During the early 1900's, there was also a gas station located on the corner of Sheridan and Hurlbut Streets.

My Grandmother Mildred or Millie, married Arthur Staley about 1911. Arthur's father, Martin Staley, had homesteaded on what is now Ferry Road on the peninsula north of East Jordan. The family lived in a house on Petoskey Avenue when my father was born. They took over the family business at 401 Antrim Street in Charlevoix in 1929, just at the start of the Great Depression. My Father, Kenneth, was 7 years old in 1929. For 20 years, Arthur & Millie operated the neighborhood grocery store. My Grandfather Arthur had been a butcher in Detroit area during the early years of their marriage and in 1929, as the Great Depression was ensuing, became proprietor of Staley's Grocery Store. They raised two daughters and a son.

Their elder daughter, Audrey Staley Hilliker, with her husband Harvey, raised a daughter Janet who currently lives in Grand Rapids. Audrey is responsible for the major editing of great grandfather's manuscript. She painstakingly compared his handwritten stories with the typed format that was prepared by his sister in law, Bertha Knowles Smith. Aunt Audrey checked the manuscript for accuracy by researching many documents and sources. She had hoped to have the manuscript published in the mid 1980's but was unable to find a Historical Society that was interested in underwriting the project.

The second daughter, Dorothy Staley Richards, with her husband Freborn "Tony" Richards, raised a son Lynn Richards who currently lives in Plano, Texas. Lynn has two sons, Christopher Richards and Tad Richards who both live in the St. Louis, Missouri area. Tad has a son Jordan, currently a US Marine, and a daughter Jenna.

From Left: Mildred Smith Staley, Stephen Horatio Smith, Dorothy Staley Richards, Lynn Freborn Richards. Circa 1940.

My father, Kenneth Arthur Staley, third child and only son of Arthur and Mildred (Smith) Staley, became proprietor of the family business in the early 1950's after serving in the US Marines in WWII. He married my mother, Arlene Hayden Staley, on August 5, 1949. Arlene's family had a farm on "the Peninsula" north of East Jordan. Together they ran the family business for over 30 years. Many people have fond memories of "Staley Grocery" on Antrim Street as it served the neighborhood with fresh meats, groceries, milk, beer & wine for over 63 years.

My sisters and I were all raised at 401 Antrim Street, a home that is attached to the store and a home that my father, with his parents and sisters, moved into in 1929. My parents still are living there! My husband David Heeres and I have a son Scott and a daughter Carrie. Scott currently lives in Colorado with his wife Kristen (Murphy), son Aiden and twin daughters Emilia and Eliana. Carrie and her husband Dan Elzinga live in Grand Rapids, Michigan and have a son Henry.

My sister Marian Staley VanKoevering lives in Fremont, Michigan with her husband Gary. My sister Martha Staley lives in Charlotte, North Carolina.

Brookside Cemetery in Charlevoix is the final resting place for my ancestors. William Smith, grandfather of Stephen; Thomas, father of Stephen; Stephen & wife Hattie; daughter Mildred Smith Staley & husband Arthur Staley. My Aunts Audrey (Harvey Hilliker) & Dorothy (Freborn "Tony" Richards) are also buried there. All of Stephen's siblings were born in Northern Michigan. His children, grandchildren, some great grandchildren and some great great grandchildren were born in Charlevoix! A very long history of the Smith family in Charlevoix.

In preparing this manuscript for publication, I have thought long and hard about what message I wanted to give. First, my great grandfather was a wonderful story teller. In spite of his lack of formal education, a fact that really saddened him, he could tell a story that holds the reader's interest and attention. Second, he felt that the history books had been altered with the date of the Battle of Pine River. You may ask, "What difference does it make after all this time?" Well, Grandpa Stevie felt that "King" Strang altered facts because he could (on his printing press) to make himself look better. He was running for re-election to the State House of Representatives in 1856 and certainly the skirmish would be less controversial if it were in the past, rather than recent, history. Grandfather also wanted to be remembered as a man of integrity. He was able to describe events and places with minute details. He took great pride in his life's events and took care to record some of them for us to read. Therefore, it is important that his story is told.

I hope you enjoy ***Footprints in the Sand***.

Donna L. Heeres
2010

About the Artist
Linda Postmus

Linda Postmus grew up in rural mid-Michigan. She studied photography, and art and life drawing at Grand Rapids Community College and studied portraiture with renowned artist Daniel Greene. During 2010, some of her work is on exhibit at the Valdez Alaska Museum where she currently resides.

Linda specializes in portraits in pastel, but also works in watercolor, oil and ink. The four illustrations she provides for this book are done in ink and only one color of paint – gray watercolor. The illustrations depict the family aboard the Schooner Michigan, Stephen learning to read, Stephen and his father in the cooper shop and Stephen on his pony delivering gold pieces to the Indians.

Linda also is an accomplished photographer. Her photos were chosen to illustrate a migrant census report for the State of Michigan. The report is quoted: "Linda's photography is influenced by her experience as a portrait painter and her compassion and appreciation for her subjects."

•••

Cover Photographs by
Donna L. Heeres

Cover Design & Book Layout by
Laurie Lesser Hodgson
North Bays Design Group, LLC

MORMON PRINT SHOP

This building was erected in 1850 by James Strang and his followers. Here during the 1850s, these Mormon dissenters published religious works and two newspapers, the *Northern Islander* and the *Daily Northern Islander*. Strang's group had settled on Beaver Island in 1846 after breaking away from the Mormons led by Brigham Young. In 1850 Strang was declared "king" of his community which made up the majority of the population on the island. In 1856 Strang was fatally shot by two disenchanted followers. In the wake of the assassination, an angry mob from the mainland stormed Beaver Island destroying buildings and forcing the Mormons to flee. At that time, this print shop was ransacked. It later became a boardinghouse. Today it serves as the headquarters for the Beaver Island Historical Society.

The old Mormon Print Shop in St. James, Beaver Island, now houses the Historical Society Museum.

Book Order Information

Footprints in the Sand may be purchased from many northwest Michigan book sellers and gift shops.

More information about Footprints in the Sand can be found on its own Facebook page with photos, information about the book, ordering information and updates.

For revisions and additions to the first printing (that are included in this second printing), please contact Donna L. Heeres to have them mailed.

Additional copies of Footprints in the Sand may be ordered directly from Donna L. Heeres by contacting her at heeres50@hotmail.com or 6323 East Jordan Road, Ellsworth, Michigan 49729.

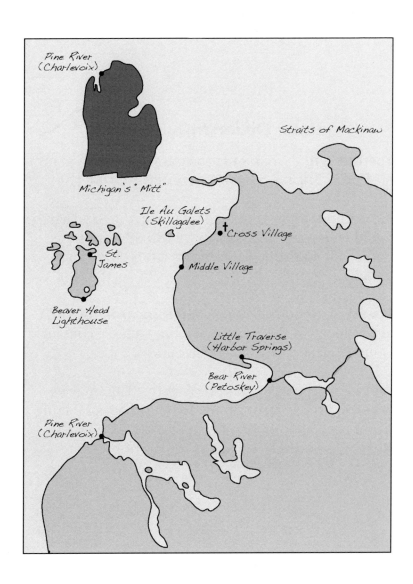

Pine River
(Charlevoix)

Straits of Mackinaw

Michigan's "Mitt"

Ile Au Galets
(Skillagalee)

✝ Cross Village

St.
James

Middle Village

Beaver Head
Lighthouse

Little Traverse
(Harbor Springs)

Bear River
(Petoskey)

Pine River
(Charlevoix)